# MACHINE LEARNING

## WITH PYTHON

*A Step by Step Guide
to Learn Machine Learning
with Python for Beginners*

Brian Walker

# Table of Contents

# Introduction

L earning is a difficult word to define since there are numerous processes included within that term. If you look in dictionary for the meaning of the word learning, you will come across numerous phrases like, "to gain knowledge, understanding of or skill, through study, experience or instruction," and "the change in behavioral tendencies through experience." A machine learns much in the same way. This book will help you understand how you can make a machine learn, and you will realize that machines learn in the same way as human beings do.

Machine learning and animal or human learning could be unrelated spheres, but they are intertwined. Many techniques that are used in machine learning have been derived from techniques human beings use to learn. The many advancements and discoveries in machine learning will always help a social scientist understand some aspects of biological learning.

You can confidently say that any change made to the structure of the machine, the data composition, or the data stored in the machine to improve the performance and accuracy of a machine is a sign of learning. When you try to better understand the concept of machine learning, you will realize that only some of these changes can be categorized as machine learning. For instance, let us look at a machine that is being used to forecast the weather in a specific region for a specific time frame. If the data related to the weather of the region in the previous year is fed into the memory of the machine, then the machine can learn from this input and it enables the machine to come up with more accurate weather predictions. This is an instance of machine learning.

Over the course of this book, you will gather information about what machine learning is, and the different techniques used in training a machine. You will also gather information about how you can build a machine learning model in Python. The book will provide information on the different algorithms that are used in machine learning, and will also help you understand how you can build a machine learning model using those algorithms. An important step during the process of building a machine learning model is to clean the data. This book will also help you understand how you can do this using the different libraries available in Python.

So, without further ado, let us begin.

# Chapter 1

# What is Machine Learning?

In today's world, we cannot live without technology in our lives. In fact, with all the rapid changes in technology these days, machines enabled with artificial intelligence are now responsible for different tasks like prediction, recognition, diagnosis, and so on.

Data is added or fed to the machines, and these machines "learn" from this data. This data is referred to as training data because it is literally used to train the machines.

Once the machines have this data, they start to analyze any patterns present within the data and then perform actions based on these patterns. Machines use various learning mechanisms for analyzing the data according to the actions that they need to perform. These learning mechanisms can now be classified into supervised and unsupervised machine learning. A newer mechanism called, "reinforcement learning," has now been introduced into the machine learning domain.

People often wonder why machines have not been designed to cater to specific tasks. It may make sense to develop a machine to cater to one problem, but how many machines do you think will need to be built in order to carry out different tasks? It is for this reason that it is important to help a machine learn. As mentioned earlier, machine learning also helps social scientists understand more about human learning. Machine learning is essential since it helps to improve the efficiency and the performance of other machines.

Here is a real-life example that will help you understand this concept better.

Let us assume that there are two random users, A and B, who love listening to music and we have access to their history of songs. If you were a music company, then you can use machine learning to understand the types of songs each of these users prefers and thereby you can come up with different ways in which you can sell your products to them.

For instance, you have access to noting down the different attributes of songs like their tempo, frequency, or the gender of the voice, and then use all these attributes and plot a graph. Once you plot a graph, over time, it will become evident that user A tends to prefer to listen to songs that have a fast tempo and are sung by male artists, whereas user B likes to listen to slow songs sung by female artists, or any other similar insight. Once you obtain this data, you can transfer it to your marketing and advertising teams to make better product decisions.

At present, we have free access to all the historical data that has been collected since the advent of technology. Not only do we have access to this data, but we can now store and process large quantities of it. Technology has certainly evolved, and it has come a long way when you look at the way we can now handle such operations. Technology is so refined these days that it provides access to more data to mine from.

Let us look at why machine learning is important:

1. Even with all the progress that engineers keep making, there will always be some tasks that are incapable of being defined explicitly.

2. There are some tasks that must be explained to the machines with the help of examples. The idea is to train the machine with the input of data and then teach it to process it to produce an output. In this manner, the machine will be aware of how it needs to deal with similar inputs of data in the future and process them accordingly to generate the appropriate outputs.

3. Data mining and machine learning are closely knit. The former refers to the process of sifting through large volumes of data to identify the necessary relationships and correlations that exist within the data set.

4. It helps the machine identify the necessary information from a large data set. There are many occasions where it is

impossible for a human being to design a machine with a set of specific conditions within which a machine can function well.

5. For most machines, the external conditions tend to have an adverse effect on the performance. In these situations, it is good to use machine learning to acclimatize the machine to the environment since this ensures that the system maintains its efficiency. Machine learning will also help the machine adapt to changes in the environment.

6. Many problems can arise if a programmer has to hardcode an elaborate process into the system; it is possible that the programmer may miss a few details. When there is a manual error in the code, it becomes very difficult for the programmer to encode the program all over again into the system. In these instances, it is best to allow the machine to learn the process.

7. The technology industry is constantly changing, and every new change gives rise to a new language that can be used as well. It does not make sense to redesign a system simply because a new change has been made in the industry, especially when many changes are being made. It is in these instances that machine learning helps the system acclimatize to these changes.

## Applications of Machine Learning

Machine learning helps to change how businesses work and operate in today's world. Through machine learning, large volumes of data can be extracted, which makes it easier for the user to draw some predictions from a data set.

There are numerous manual tasks that one cannot complete within a stipulated time frame if the task includes the analysis of large volumes of data. Machine learning is the solution to such issues. In the modern world, we are overwrought with large volumes of data and information, and there is no way a human being can process that information. Therefore, there is a need to automate such processes, and machine learning helps with that.

When any analysis or discovery is automated fully, it will become easier to obtain the necessary information from that analysis. This will also help the engineer automate any future processes. The world of business analytics, data science, and big data requires machine learning and deep learning. Business intelligence and predictive learning are no longer restricted to just large businesses but are accessible to small companies and businesses too. This allows a small business to utilize the information that it has collected effectively. This section covers some of the applications of machine learning in the real world.

### Virtual Personal Assistants

Some examples of virtual assistants are Allo, Google Now, Siri and Alexa. These tools help users access necessary information through voice commands. All you must do is activate the assistant, and you can ask the machine any questions you want.

Your personal assistant will look for the necessary information based on your question, and then provide you with an answer. You can also use this assistant to perform regular tasks like setting reminders or alarms. Machine learning is an important part of this tool since it helps the system gather the necessary information to provide you with an answer.

### Density Estimation

Machine learning will help a system use any data that is available on the Internet, and it can use that data to predict or suggest some information to users. For example, if you want to purchase a copy of "A Song of Ice and Fire" from a book store, and run it through a machine, you can generate a similar copy of the book using that very machine.

### Latent Variables

When you work with latent variables, the machine will try to identify if these variables are related to other data points and variables within the data set. This is a handy method when you use a data set where it is difficult to identify the relationship between different variables. There are times when you will be unable to identify why there is a change in a variable. The engineer can understand the data better if he or she can take a look at the different latent variables within the data set.

### *Reduction of Dimensionality*

The data set that is used to train machines to predict the outcome to any problem will have some dimensions and variables. If there are over three dimensions within the data set, it will become impossible for the human mind to visualize or understand that data. In these situations, it is always good to have a machine learning model to reduce the volume of the data into smaller segments that are easily manageable. This will help the user identify the relationships that exist within the data set.

Every machine learning model will ensure that the machine learns from the data that is provided to it. The machine can then be used to classify data or predict the outcome or the result for a specific problem. It can also be used in numerous applications like self-driving cars. Machine learning models help to improve the ability of smartphones to recognize the user's face or the way in which Google Home or Alexa can recognize your accent and voice and how the accuracy of the machines improves if they have been learning for longer.

## Advantages and Disadvantages of Machine Learning

The disadvantages of machine learning are:

1. In any machine learning technique, we always train the model using a training data set and then validate that model using a testing data set. The model is then used on newer data sets to predict the outcome. It becomes difficult for one to identify if there is a bias in the model that has been created, and if there is a bias in the model, the inferences made will be incorrect.

2. Social scientists will start relying only on machine learning to solve problems. Therefore, it is important that some improvements and changes should be made to supervised machine learning algorithms to improve the performance of the model.

Some of the advantages of machine learning are:

1. When businesses perform analyses, they use large volumes of data, and they prefer using real-time data to perform those analyses. It is difficult for human beings to analyze that volume of data. Therefore, machine learning makes it easier to analyze with ease.

2. Machine learning is improving day by day. Now that most engineers are integrating machine learning with deep learning, they are reducing the cost of data engineering and data pre-processing.

## Steps in Building a Machine Learning System

Regardless of the type of model that you are trying to build or the problem that you are trying to solve, you will follow the steps mentioned in this section while building a machine learning algorithm.

### *Define Objective*

The first step, as it is with any other task that you perform, is to define the purpose or the objective you want to accomplish using your system. This is an important step since the data you will collect, the algorithm you use, and many other factors depend on this objective.

### *Collect Data*

Once you have your objective in mind, you should collect the required data. It is a time-consuming process, but it is the next important step that you must achieve. You should collect the relevant data and ensure that it is the right data for the problem you are trying to solve.

### *Prepare Data*

This is another important step, but engineers often overlook it. If you do overlook this step, you will be making a mistake. It is only when the input data is clean and relevant that you will obtain an accurate result or prediction.

### Select Algorithm

Numerous algorithms can be used to solve a problem, including Structured Vector Machine (SVM), k-nearest, Naive-Bayes and Apriori, etc. You must choose the algorithm that best suits the objective.

### Train Model

When your data set is ready, you should feed it into the system and help the machine learn using the chosen algorithm.

### Test Model

When your model is trained, and you believe that it has provided the relevant results, you can test the accuracy of the model using a test data set.

### Predict

The model will perform numerous iterations with the training data set and the test data set. You can look at the predictions and provide feedback to the model to help it improve the predictions that it makes.

### Deploy

Once you have tested the model and are happy with how it works, you can sterilize that model and integrate it into any application that you want to use. This means that the model that you have developed can now be deployed.

The steps followed will vary depending on the type of application and algorithm that you are using. You can choose to use a supervised or unsupervised machine learning algorithm. The steps mentioned in this section are often the steps followed by most engineers when they are developing a machine learning algorithm. There are numerous tools and functions that you can use to build a machine learning model. This book will help you with understanding more about how you can design a machine learning model using Python.

# Chapter 2

# Machine Learning - Concepts & Terms

As mentioned in the previous chapter, machine learning is a process where the engineer will train the machine to predict the outcome of any problem. The engineer will feed the machine with some training data sets to help the machine learn. A system without any artificial intelligence will not be able to interpret the outcome for a new data set, but it can provide the output to any input that is provided to it. Systems with artificial intelligence take it one step further where they can learn, predict, and improve the results. These systems can do this because they learn.

Let us try to understand how children learn to identify objects, and how they associate an object with a word. Let us assume that there is a bowl of apples and oranges on the table. You, as an adult or parent, will introduce the round and red object as an apple, and the other object as an orange. In this example, the words apple and orange are labels, and the shapes and colors are attributes. You can train the machine, in the same way, using a set of attributes and labels. The machine will classify the object using the attributes that it was given as the input.

Machine learning models that use labeled data are called supervised machine learning models. When you were in school or college, your progress report or grades would indicate your progress, and your professors or teachers are giving you that feedback. In the same way, you as an engineer can give the machine feedback regardless of what type of machine learning method you are using to train the machine.

Let us look at an input example – [red, round]. Based on what the machine and child were told, they will relate a red and round object to an apple. Now, place a red cricket ball in front of both the child and the machine. When it comes to the machine, you should give it a negative response if it does not give you the required output. This means that you should monitor the predictions that the machine is making about the object. If you want to include a few more attributes to help the machine identify the object correctly, you can do this too. The machine will only learn in this manner. It is also for this reason that when you spend time training the machine using a high-quality data set, the machine will learn to produce accurate results.

This is an example of a simple classification model in the machine learning ecosystem. The next chapters in this book will introduce you to some complex models and systems that will help you understand how the machine can learn to differentiate between an apple and a cricket ball, although both of these objects are red and round.

Before we proceed to learn more about machine learning, let us first understand the differences between machine learning, artificial intelligence, and deep learning.

## Machine Learning, Artificial Intelligence, and Deep Learning

The terms machine learning, artificial intelligence, and deep learning are often used interchangeably, but these terms do not mean the same thing.

Data scientists and engineers use artificial intelligence to help a machine behave like a human being. The objective of artificial intelligence is to ensure that a machine can perfectly mimic human behavior. Some examples of machines with artificial intelligence are IBM's Watson and Deep Blue Chess.

As defined in the previous chapter, machine learning is the use of mathematical and statistical models to help a machine predict the outcome or the result of any problem. The machine does this by using historical data.

Deep learning is a subset of machine learning, and an engineer uses different algorithms and functions in deep learning to help a machine learn by itself. The machine will learn to use the correct methods to obtain the required output. Natural language processing and neural networks are a part of the deep learning ecosystem.

## Objectives of Machine Learning System

The system of machine learning usually has one of the following objectives.

### *Predict a category*

This type of machine learning model will help the engineer or data scientist analyze the input data set and predict the category that the data set will fall into. In these models, the prediction is often a binary answer. For example, this type of model can be used to answer questions like "Will it rain today?" or "Is this object a fruit?" The model achieves this by using some input data as a base to learn. Once it learns, it can be used to categorize or classify the data into different categories. This process is termed as classification.

### *Predict a quantity*

This type of system is often used to predict any value. For example, it can be used to predict when it may rain, and also predict numerous attributes like the percentage of humidity, temperature, relative humidity, air pressure, etc. This is a regression based problem, and numerous regression algorithms can be used to predict the output.

### *Anomaly Detector Systems*

An anomaly detector system helps the user identify any outliers in the data set. This type of system is often used in the e-commerce or banking industry where the objective is to identify and flag an unusual or fraudulent transaction. This helps the business avoid or prevent any losses.

### *Clustering Systems*

Many engineers and data scientists are still working on perfecting a clustering system, but there are numerous applications to using these systems since they can change the way a business is conducted. In these types of systems, the user is always categorized into a cluster based on some attributes like their age, sex, region they live in, products they purchase, movies they like to watch, etc. By using a clustering system, a business can suggest to the user different programs or movies they may like to watch based on the cluster that the user falls into.

# Chapter 3

# Types of Machine Learning

## Supervised Machine Learning

Supervised machine learning algorithms use the training data set to help a machine learn. This training data set will contain different input and output variable sets, and these sets are known as supervisory signals. An engineer uses this type of learning if he or she wants to generate or predict the output using a pre-existing function. If the data set is discrete, the function is called a classifier, and if the data set is continuous, the function is called a regressor. Every supervised machine learning algorithm has a generalized method that the machine can use to obtain or predict the desired output. The supervised machine learning algorithm works in the following manner:

### *Step 1*

Once the engineer has identified the problem, he or she should determine the different examples, which can be used to help the machine learn. The engineer should also be extremely careful about the training data set that is being used since the machine will only learn from that data set.

## Step 2

The engineer should identify the correct data set that can be used to solve the problem and scrub the data so it can be used to train the machine. The data set that the engineer uses should include all possible functions and outputs that the machine should look at. The engineer should also ensure that every input variable is mapped to the corresponding output variable.

## Step 3

In this step, the engineer should choose the input data set that they should provide to the machine. It is important to provide the right data set to the machine since this will affect the performance of the model. The input variables used are provided in the form of a vector, and this vector possesses all the information about the characteristics and properties of the input variable. The engineer must then teach the machine how it should choose the necessary variables to obtain the desired output. If the machine cannot identify the right variables to use, it will provide incorrect outputs.

## Step 4

It is only the engineer who can decide what the structure of the function can be. This function is dependent on the data set being used. The engineer should feed this function to the machine to help it obtain the required output.

*Step 5*

The engineer should now complete the design of the model. To do this, the engineer should first run the algorithm on the data set. He or she can also enter different parameters to control the working of the algorithm. Experts recommend that an engineer should use cross-validation methods to estimate the output. With this technique, the data set is split into small subsets, which makes it easy to estimate the parameters.

*Step 6*

When the algorithm runs, and the machine generates a function, the engineer can identify a way to test the performance and the accuracy of the model. For this purpose, the engineer can use a testing data set and verify if the model performs well and predicts the right outcome.

Numerous supervised machine learning algorithms can be used to solve different problems, and each of these algorithms has its respective pros and cons. It is important that the engineer chooses the correct algorithm to solve a problem.

## Unsupervised Machine Learning

Unsupervised machine learning algorithms are different from supervised machine learning algorithms in the sense that the former will help the machine learn how to predict the outcome using a data set without any labels. These algorithms cannot be applied to regression and classification problems since you do not let the machine know what the output should be. It is for this reason that it becomes difficult to train the machine in the usual manner. These algorithms are often used to uncover the underlying relationships and structure within the data set.

### *Uses of unsupervised machine learning algorithms*

You can derive the approximation of results for any data set using supervised machine learning algorithms. As mentioned earlier, an unsupervised machine learning algorithm helps to uncover the underlying relationship within the data set. It is hard to determine if the result obtained is accurate since you are unaware of what the outcome should be. It is for this reason that most engineers prefer using supervised machine learning algorithms for real-world problems.

If the data set provided does not have sufficient data, you should use an unsupervised machine learning algorithm. For instance, you can use an unsupervised machine learning algorithm if you want to identify the right time to launch a new product into the market. If you want to learn more about your customer base, you should use a supervised machine learning algorithm.

There are many applications or uses of unsupervised machine learning algorithms:

1. Since most data have numerous variables, the clustering algorithm helps to split the data into multiple data sets based on the similarity that exists between these variables. Cluster analysis does tend to overestimate the similarities that exist between different variables in the data set. It is for this

reason that most engineers do not choose to perform cluster analysis on their data sets, especially if they are looking to create customer segments.

2. You can also identify any irregularities within the data set using anomaly detection. This allows different companies to identify fraudulent transactions, identify faulty hardware or tools, or even identify outliers or errors due to human prediction.

3. You can identify the different types of items that occur in the data set using association mining. Retailers often use this approach when they perform basket analysis since that allows them to identify the list of items that a specific customer or a group of customers purchase at a specific point in time. This will allow the retailer to work on various branding and marketing strategies.

4. You can use different latent variable models if you want to reduce the number of features within the data set or if you want to break the data set into different components.

5. You can implement a supervised machine learning algorithm based on the information that you obtain from an unsupervised machine learning algorithm. For example, an unsupervised machine learning algorithm can be used to identify the clusters within a data set. These clusters can be used as additional input while developing a supervised machine learning algorithm.

## Reinforcement Learning

Reinforcement learning is another branch of machine learning, and in this type of learning, the machine works towards maximizing the reward it receives by performing the right action in any situation. Many engineers use this type of learning where they allow a machine to identify the right behavior or action that it should take in any situation. Reinforcement learning and supervised machine learning is very different. The latter gives the machine a training data set, which also provides the required output to the machine. The former does not give the machine any answers. The machine should decide what it must do to obtain the results. The machine will only learn from its own experiences since there is no training data provided.

In the example below, there is a reward and there is an agent. There are many obstacles placed between the machine or agent, and the reward. The machine or agent should identify the right path that it should take to reach the reward in the shortest time possible. The image below will provide some information about this problem:

Image - (Bajaj, n.d.)

In the image above, there is a robot, which is the machine or agent, the fire that represents the obstacles and the diamond, which represents the reward. The robot should look for the different ways it can reach the diamond while avoiding fire. The aim should be to reach the diamond in the shortest time possible. The robot is rewarded for every correct step taken, and for every incorrect step it takes the reward is reduced. The total reward is calculated when the robot finally reaches the diamond.

## *Reinforcement Learning Process*

This section will shed some light on the process of reinforcement learning:

**Input**: The start from where the model begins to run is called the input.

**Output**: Since there are many solutions to a problem, the model can choose or predict different outputs.

**Training**: The model is trained based on the input data that is being taken to solve the problem. The engineer or the user can choose to reward or punish the model depending on the output that is returned to the user.

**Learning**: The model will learn from every reward.

**Solution**: Based on the reward that the model receives, it will decide the best solution that it should follow to solve the problem.

## *Types of Reinforcement*

There are two types of reinforcement learning.

### Positive

The model will always try to maximize the strength and frequency of a behavior that leads to a specific event. This means that this type of learning will always give the model a positive experience. The advantages of positive reinforcement learning are:

- The model will learn to adapt to any changes or updates made to the data set.

- Improves the performance and accuracy of the model.

The disadvantages of this type of learning are:

- If the model is rewarded too many times, it will result in an overload in all the states.

### Negative

Negative reinforcement learning helps the model strengthen the behavior that helps to prevent a negative outcome. The advantages of this type of learning are:

- Improves the performance of the model by allowing it to defy a method.

- It will increase the frequency of the behavior.

The disadvantages of this type of learning are:

- This will allow the model just to provide enough to meet the minimum behavior.

# Chapter 4

# Why Use Python for Machine Learning

Python has certainly become one of the most popular machine languages in the world because it is quite easy to use and is efficient. The simplicity and the readability of Python make it easily understandable. Also, it is considered to be one of the most beginner-friendly languages. The vast number of libraries and packages available certainly make it easy to achieve complex functions with minimum coding.

Applications of machine learning usually work with vast data sets and inbuilt libraries like Numpy SciPy, TensorFlow. All this makes it easy to develop applications for machine learning and deep learning.

Python can also be extended to work for different programs and that's why data scientists are using it to analyze data. Learning to code in Python is a good idea since it will help you analyze and interpret the data to identify solutions that will work efficiently for you. Python can work across various devices and it is designed using clean and simple syntax- thereby making it intuitive and easy to learn for the users.

Guido van Rossum developed this high-level language during the late 1980s and this is quite popular within the developer community regardless of the stage of the coder.

## Simple and Easy to Learn

As mentioned earlier, Python was developed to be a simple and minimalistic language. So, any program that's coded in Python will look like a pseudo code in English. This is the feature that makes Python an easily understandable program for anyone. The syntax and the keywords used in it are more usually in English. The quality of this language is such that it allows the programmer to concentrate on problem-solving instead of worrying about learning the syntax and how to use it. All this baggage is usually associated with several other high-level languages.

## High-level Language

A high-level language means that from a developer's perspective, various internal details like memory management are abstracted from you and are then automatically taken care of by the language. This is the best high-level language for a non-programmer to learn.

## Fast and Efficient to Use

Python is incredibly quick to act when it comes to the execution of actions and this is another feature that makes Python a powerful language. Any program that is written in Python can be embedded

29

and executed just like a script within programs coded in other languages like C or C++. You can also write a simple Python script and then use it to execute any other C/C++ programs.

## Open Source

Since this language is an open source, it is available free of cost. It essentially means that you can write and distribute a code written in Python. The code of Python is well-maintained so it can be constantly reused and improved upon by developed all over the world.

## Interpreted

Similar to Java, even Python is an interpreted language. It means that any program that's coded in Python doesn't have to be compiled every time it must be executed. Instead, it merely needs to be compiled once and then it can be executed on various devices. For instance, if a program is written in C or C++ that's compiler based, it gets converted from the source code (into a format that humans can read) to binary code (0's and 1's of the machine language) using different flags and options that are platform specific. This binary code must then be fed into the device's memory using a linker or a loader and then it can start running. This linker, loader or compiler is an additional overhead that can be easily avoided by using a language like Python. Python doesn't compile the source code into a binary format and it is designed in such a manner that it can be directly executed from the source code itself.

The source code is internally converted into an intermediate form referred to as the bytecode. The machine then interprets the bytecode before it can be executed. This feature makes Python quite a powerful language and sets it apart from all other computer languages. This allows the user to create the code once and then use the same code across different devices without having to worry about compilation or library linking overloads. You merely need to copy the program files to the concerned device and then start working.

## Object Oriented

As with any other modern language, even Python has an object-oriented approach towards programming. The code is organized in classes that are referred to as templates and "objects" is an example of such a class. Objects are the building blocks of an object-oriented programming language- it effectively combines data along with the methods that are used to perform any functions on this data.

## Portable

As mentioned earlier, one of the reasons why Python is a great language to learn is not just its simplicity but also its design. It is designed in such a way that it can work on multiple platforms that require any new changes when transferring between devices. As long as you take proper care, Python is quite portable.

There are different platforms on which Python code can be used like Windows, Solaris, Macintosh, FreeBSD, VMS, Palm OS, Linux, VxWorks, and even PlayStation!

## Batteries Included

When it comes to Python, it isn't merely about the speed of the execution but also about the speed of writing the code. Various inbuilt libraries and data types assist the system in completing complex operations. For all this, Python requires fewer lines of code than any other language. So, the job of the programmer is certainly made a lot easier. This feature of pre-loaded libraries is bundled up with Python and is referred to as "batteries included."

The Python library is so massive that it allows the programmer to concentrate on thinking about solutions to problems instead of worrying about how to implement the data structures or any other low-level details that are involved in the process of problem-solving. The libraries pretty much cover anything and everything from working with databases to HTML to audio files to Graphical User Interface to the security (uses cryptography) and everything else in between.

Using Python enables the programmer to concentrate on the process of machine learning and the objective of the system all thanks to the highly efficient in-built libraries of Python, which take care of the implementation process.

Python offers an end-to-end solution to build a system of machine learning right from wrangling data to feature extraction, modeling, training and evaluating these systems for visualization. To create a data pipeline, a program must be easily integrated with BigQuery, Kafka, pubsub, redshift, etc., and Python precisely does this. Data wrangling can be easily achieved using Panda, Numpy and Pyspark, which in turn can be integrated with several other big data engines (Dask is Python's big data engine).

**Numpy, Panda and Scikit-learn**

Python offers a large inbuilt image and video library that come handy while dealing with the feature extraction phase. This feature makes Python desirable and easy to use language for machine learning.

The Scikit-learn package also helps in different stages of building a machine learning model; training the model and evaluating the system, thereby making the whole pipeline come together seamlessly. Pytorch is a good alternative for beginners.

Once you use all of this to build, train and test the machine, Python offers an easy deployment option. Creating a REST-API and a serializing model is quite simple when you use Python.

The philosophy of Python is based on minimalism. This minimalistic approach gives clear syntaxes and English-like words that enable the completion of a given task within fewer lines of code when compared to any other language. The code is easily readable too and easy to work with.

# Chapter 5

# Data Scrubbing and Preparation

Before you build a machine learning model, you should collect the data and prepare it to ensure that it can be used to train the machine. This is not enjoyable work, but it is essential that you do this so your model is accurate. Engineers often spend hours writing code before they realize that there is something amiss with the data. It is for this reason that experts mention that it is important to clean and scrub the data before it is used to train a model.

Many companies have teams dedicated to cleaning the data that they have collected, but there are many companies that do not worry about this. It is for this reason that most analyses performed using unclean data do not provide accurate results. The goal of any engineer should first be to clean the data, or at least try to clean it to the best of their ability.

## Quickly Check Your Data

When you obtain any data set, new or old, you should always verify the contents in that data set using the .head() method.

```
import pandas as pd
df = pd.read_csv('path_to_data')
df.head(10)
>>
```

You will receive some output when you run the above code. This will help you ensure that the data has been picked up from the correct file. You should now look at the types and names of the different columns in the data set. More often than not you will receive data that is not exactly what you are looking for like dates, strings, and other incomprehensible information. Therefore, it is important that you look for these oddities in the beginning.

```
#Get column names
column_names = df.columns
print(column_names)
#Get column data types
df.dtypes
#Also check if the column is unique
for i in column_names:
print('{} is unique: {}'.format(i, df[i].is_unique))
```

You should now look for the index that is associated with the data frame. You can do this by calling on the function called '.index.' You will receive the following error if there is no index attached to the data frame: AttributeError: 'function' object has no attribute 'index.'

#Check the index values

df.index.values

#Check if a certain index exists

'foo' in df.index.values

#If index does not exist

df.set_index('column_name_to_use', inplace=True)

You have now checked most of the data, and are aware of the data types. You will also know if there are any duplicates in the columns in the data set and whether an index has been assigned to the data frame. The next step is to identify the columns that you want to include in your analysis and the columns that you want to get rid of. In the example below we are trying to get rid of the columns that have the indices 1, 3, and 5. For this purpose, we will add the string values to the list which will help us drop the columns.

#Create list comprehension of the columns you want to lose

columns_to_drop = [column_names[i] for i in [1, 3, 5]]

#Drop unwanted columns

df.drop(columns_to_drop, inplace=True, axis=1)

The statement inplace=True has been included in the code to save the file faster. This means that you do not need to save the updated file again. Since most functions and packages in pandas allow you to use the inplace=True statement, you should make the most out of it.

**What To Do With NaN?**

If you want to identify a way to fill in the blank data or remove any errors in the data set, you should use the two methods dropna() and fillna(). The process of filling blank data and getting rid of errors becomes faster when you use these two methods. That being said, you must ensure that you document every step that you perform so another user can easily understand what it is that you are trying to achieve by writing the code.

You can fill the NaN values with the mean or median value of all the numbers or with strings depending on the data type. Many engineers are still unsure of what they can do with malformed or missing data. This is because the engineer must decide what to do with the data set depending on the type of analysis that he or she is performing.

Experts suggest that engineers use their best judgment or speak to the people they are working with to decide on whether they should remove blank data or fill it using a default value.

#Fill NaN with ' '

df['col'] = df['col'].fillna(' ')

#Fill NaN with 99

df['col'] = df['col'].fillna(99)

#Fill NaN with the mean of the column

df['col'] = df['col'].fillna(df['col'].mean())

Alternatively, you can choose to move the non-null values backward or forward by using the following statement: method ='pad.' This statement is used as an argument for a method. This argument can be used to fill in values in blank cells or data spaces with the preceding information. You can choose to fill one empty cell or many empty cells by defining the limit. Regardless of what you are doing, ensure that you fill in the information correctly.

df = pd.DataFrame(data={'col1':[np.nan, np.nan, 2,3,4, np.nan, np.nan]})

    col1

0  NaN

1  NaN

2  2.0

3  3.0

4  4.0 #This is the value to fill forward

5  NaN

6  NaN

df.fillna(method='pad', limit=1)

    col1

0  NaN

1  NaN

2  2.0

3  3.0

4  4.0

5  4.0 #Filled forward

6  NaN

If you look at the above code and the output, you will notice that the data was only filled in the data frame where the index was 5. If there was no limit placed on 'pad,' the full data frame would have been filled. Not only are we limiting forward filling, but we are also using the method bfill to limit backward filling.

#Fill the first two NaN values with the first available value

df.fillna(method='bfill')

   col1

0  2.0 #Filled

1  2.0 #Filled

2  2.0

3  3.0

4  4.0

5  NaN

6  NaN

You can also choose to drop those values from the data frame looking at their rows or columns.

#Drop any rows which have any nans

df.dropna()

#Drop columns that have any nans

df.dropna(axis=1)

#Only drop columns which have at least 90% non-NaNs

df.dropna(thresh=int(df.shape[0] * .9), axis=1)

Alternatively, you can choose to drop a column depending on the number of non-null variables present in a column. You can do this by using the parameter thresh=N.

**Dedupe**

Dedupe is a library which uses machine learning to identify duplicates in a data set. We will be using the Chicago Early Childhood Location data set for the examples in this section.

#Columns and the number of missing values in each

Id has 0 na values

Source has 0 na values

Site name has 0 na values

Address has 0 na values

Zip has 1333 na values

Phone has 146 na values

Fax has 3299 na values

Program Name has 2009 na values

Length of Day has 2009 na values

IDHS Provider ID has 3298 na values

Agency has 3325 na values

Neighborhood has 2754 na values

Funded Enrollment has 2424 na values

Program Option has 2800 na values

Number per Site EHS has 3319 na values

Number per Site HS has 3319 na values

Director has 3337 na values

Head Start Fund has 3337 na values

Early Head Start Fund has 2881 na values

CC fund has 2818 na values

Progmod has 2818 na values

Website has 2815 na values

Executive Director has 3114 na values

Center Director has 2874 na values

ECE Available Programs has 2379 na values

NAEYC Valid Until has 2968 na values

NAEYC Program Id has 3337 na values

Email Address has 3203 na values

Ounce of Prevention Description has 3185 na values

Purple binder service type has 3215 na values

Column has 3337 na values

Column2 has 3018 na values

You should save the method as the cleaning package. This will make it easier for you to deal with duplicate data.

import pandas as pd

import numpy

import dedupe

import os

```python
import csv

import re

from unidecode import unidecode

def preProcess(column):

    '''

    Used to prevent errors during the dedupe process.

    '''

    try:

        column = column.decode('utf8')

    except AttributeError:

        pass

    column = unidecode(column)

    column = re.sub('  +', ' ', column)

    column = re.sub('\n', ' ', column)

    column = column.strip().strip('"').strip("'").lower().strip()


    if not column:

        column = None

    return column
```

Let us now begin to import the information in the .csv column by column when we are processing the data.

```python
def readData(filename):
    data_d = {}
    with open(filename) as f:
        reader = csv.DictReader(f)
        for row in reader:
            clean_row = [(k, preProcess(v)) for (k, v) in row.items()]
            row_id = int(row['Id'])
            data_d[row_id] = dict(clean_row)
    return df
name_of_file = 'data.csv'
print('Cleaning and importing data ... ')
df = readData(name_of_file)
```

At this point we will need to let the function know the different categories and features it would need to look at before it determines the duplicate values. The features have been denoted by the term fields in the section below, and each of these fields is assigned a data type. The output also mentions if there are any missing values in the data set. There are a list of different types that you are allowed to use here, but let us stick to rows if we want to keep things simple. We will also not look at every column to look for duplicate values. You can, however, do this if you believe it will help your cause.

#Set fields

```
fields = [

        {'field' : 'Source', 'type': 'Set'},

        {'field' : 'Site name', 'type': 'String'},

        {'field' : 'Address', 'type': 'String'},

        {'field' : 'Zip', 'type': 'Exact', 'has missing' : True},

        {'field' : 'Phone', 'type': 'String', 'has missing' : True},

        {'field' : 'Email Address', 'type': 'String', 'has missing' :
            True},

        ]
```

Let us now begin to feed the package with some information.

```
#Pass in our model

deduper = dedupe.Dedupe(fields)

#Check if it is working

deduper

>>

<dedupe.api.Dedupe at 0x11535bbe0>

#Feed some sample data in ... 15000 records

deduper.sample(df, 15000)
```

Let us now move onto the labelling part. You will prompt the dedupe package to label the data when you run this method.

```
dedupe.consoleLabel(deduper)
```

Do these records refer to the same thing?

(y)es / (n)o / (u)nsure / (f)inished

You will no longer need to search or peruse through large volumes of data to see if there is any duplication within the data frame. You can use a neural network to identify the duplicates in the data set. When you provide the network with labeled data, finish training the model, and save the progress, you can be certain that the network predicts the data correctly.

```
deduper.train()

#Save training

with open(training_file, 'w') as tf:

    deduper.writeTraining(tf)

#Save settings

with open(settings_file, 'wb') as sf:

    deduper.writeSettings(sf)
```

Now that we are almost done, we will need to identify a way to set a threshold for the data set. When the value of the variable recall_weight is one, we are asking the deduper package to be more precise or recall the value. If the value of recall_weight is greater than one, there will be more than one recall. You can always work with these settings to identify the process that works best for the model you are developing.

```
threshold = deduper.threshold(df, recall_weight=1)
```

We can now look through the data frame to identify where the duplicates exist. It is easier to do this using the model instead of doing this by hand.

#Cluster the duplicates together

clustered_dupes = deduper.match(data_d, threshold)

print('There are {} duplicate sets'.format(len(clustered_dupes)))

Let us now look at the duplicates.

clustered_dupes

>>

[((0, 1, 215, 509, 510, 1225, 1226, 1879, 2758, 3255),

array([0.88552043,  0.88552043,  0.77351897,  0.88552043, 0.88552043,

0.88552043,  0.88552043,  0.89765924,  0.75684386, 0.83023088])),

((2, 3, 216, 511, 512, 1227, 1228, 2687), ...

This does not actually say much about the data set. So, what do you think this output shows us? What has happened to all the values in the data set? If you pay close attention to these values (0, 1, 215, 509, 510, 1225, 1226, 1879, 2758, 3255), they indicate the locations for where the duplicates are. These locations are the parts where deduper thinks the values are the same. We can always look at the original data if we want to verify this.

{'Id': '215',

'Source': 'cps_early_childhood_portal_scrape.csv',

'Site name': 'salvation army temple',

'Address': '1 n. ogden',

...

{'Id': '509',

'Source': 'cps_early_childhood_portal_scrape.csv',

'Site name': 'salvation army - temple / salvation army',

'Address': '1 n ogden ave',

'Zip': None,

..

This looks like a bunch of duplicates, doesn't it? You can use deduper for many other functions like interaction fields where there is a multiplicative and not additive interaction between the fields or as a matchblock for numerous sequences.

## Matching Strings Using Fuzzywuzzy

You should always try to use this library when you are comparing strings. This is because this package gives you a score that will help you understand how similar two strings are. This is a tool that most engineers use since they can use this package to identify any issues with data validation. They can also use this tool to clean the data set or perform any analysis. This approach will only work on small data sets. That being said, you can always use fuzzywuzzy if you want to match strings in a more scientific manner. This package uses the Levenshtein distance when it compares two strings. This distance is calculated as the distance between the similarity metric of two strings. The metric is calculated as the distance between the number of edits that need to be made to characters in order to change one word into another.

For example, if you want to change the string bar into foo or vice versa, you would need to make at least three edits if you want to change one word to another. This is the Levenshtein distance. Let us see how we can do this in practice.

```
$ pip3 install fuzzywuzzy
#test.py
from fuzzywuzzy import fuzz
from fuzzywuzzy import process
foo = 'is this string'
bar = 'like that string?'
fuzz.ratio(foo, bar)
>>
71
fuzz.WRatio(foo, bar) #Weighted ratio
>>
73
fuzz.UQRatio(foo, bar) #Unicode quick ratio
>> 73
```

The fuzzywuzzy package gives you access to different functions that you can use to evaluate the strings in your data set. We will only look at the standard implementation of this logic for the purpose of this book. We will then look at tokenized strings which will return the measure of similarity between the sequences. These tokens will lie within a range of zero and hundred. The token will be sorted before it is used to compare strings. This is important since you not only want to know what the string contains, but also want to know its position.

The strings bar and foo have been allotted the same tokens, but these are different. So, you cannot expect to treat them in the same way. You can therefore look for this difference within your data set and make any adjustments if necessary.

```
foo = 'this is a foo'

bar = 'foo a is this'

fuzz.ratio(foo, bar)

>>

31

fuzz.token_sort_ratio('this is a foo', 'foo a is this')

>>

100
```

The next best thing you can do is to find the closest match from a list of values. Let us look at an example where we will be looking for Harry Potter titles. Many people do not remember the titles of all the Harry Potter books. So, they can use this method to score the books so that the machine can predict the name of the book. If you were to guess "fire," the machine will score the list and display the title with "fire" in it as the output.

```
lst_to_eval = ['Harry Potter and the Philosopher's Stone',

'Harry Potter and the Chamber of Secrets',

'Harry Potter and the Prisoner of Azkaban',

'Harry Potter and the Goblet of Fire',

'Harry Potter and the Order of the Phoenix',

'Harry Potter and the Half-Blood Prince',

'Harry Potter and the Deathly Hallows']

#Top two responses based on my guess

process.extract("fire", lst_to_eval, limit=2)

>>

[('Harry Potter and the Goblet of Fire', 60), ("Harry Potter and the Sorcerer's Stone", 30)

results = process.extract("fire", lst_to_eval, limit=2)

for result in results:

   print('{}: has a score of {}'.format(result[0], result[1]))

>>
```

Harry Potter and the Goblet of Fire: has a score of 60

Harry Potter and the Sorcerer's Stone: has a score of 30

If you want, you can return only one value.

```
>>> process.extractOne("stone", lst_to_eval)
```

("Harry Potter and the Sorcerer's Stone", 90)

In the previous section, we talked about deduping. Let us now look at a similar application of the fuzzywuzzy package. You can use a list of strings that contain duplicates and use this package to remove those duplicates. This function is not as fancy or amazing as a neural network, but it works perfectly well on small data sets.

Let us continue with the Harry Potter example. We now want to look for duplicate characters in the book using the character list. For this, you must set the threshold between zero and one hundred. Let us make the default 70. Remember that as the threshold decreases the number of duplicates in the data set will increase.

```
#List of duplicate character names

contains_dupes = [

'Harry Potter',

'H. Potter',

'Harry James Potter',

'James Potter',

'Ronald Bilius \'Ron\' Weasley',

'Ron Weasley',

'Ronald Weasley']

#Print the duplicate values
```

```
process.dedupe(contains_dupes)

>>

dict_keys(['Harry   James   Potter',   "Ronald   Bilius   'Ron'
Weasley"])
```

#Print the duplicate values with a higher threshold

```
process.dedupe(contains_dupes, threshold=90)

>>

dict_keys(['Harry James Potter', 'H. Potter', "Ronald Bilius 'Ron'
Weasley"])
```

You can also perform some fuzzywuzzy matching using the datetime package. This package will allow you to extract different dates from strings. You should use this package when you do not want to make use of the regex expression.

```
from dateutil.parser import parse

dt = parse("Today is January 1, 2047 at 8:21:00AM",
fuzzy=True)

print(dt)

>>

2047-01-01 08:21:00

dt = parse("May 18, 2049 something something", fuzzy=True)

print(dt)

>>

2049-05-18 00:00:00
```

**Try Some Sklearn**

Once you have cleaned the data, you should also prepare it well to ensure that it is in the right format. You must ensure that the data you feed the model or machine meets certain criteria. The examples used in this section are available in the documentation. It is important that you read the documentation well before you begin using sklearn since it will help you understand more about the package. The first package we will be importing is the preprocessing package. We will then add additional methods whenever necessary. You may need to check the version of sklearn on your system if there is an issue with the output. The programs in this section were written in the 0.20.0 version. We will now work with two data types, int and str, to learn more about the preprocessing technique.

```
#At start of project

from sklearn import preprocessing

#And let's create a random array of ints to process

ary_int = np.random.randint(-100, 100, 10)

ary_int

>>[  5, -41, -67,  23, -53, -57, -36, -25,  10,  17]

#And some str to work with

ary_str = ['foo', 'bar', 'baz', 'x', 'y', 'z']
```

Let us now look at how we can label the variables in the data set using the LabelEncoder function. It is important to do this since you cannot feed the model raw strings. You can definitely do that, but that is outside the scope of this book. Therefore, we will ensure that we encode the labels of every string using the values zero and one. There are six unique values in the ary_str variable, and therefore the range of values we will use to encode that data will lie between zero and one.

```
from sklearn.preprocessing import LabelEncoder

l_encoder = preprocessing.LabelEncoder()

l_encoder.fit(ary_str)

>> LabelEncoder()

#What are our values?

l_encoder.transform(['foo'])

>> array([2])

l_encoder.transform(['baz'])

>> array([1])

l_encoder.transform(['bar'])

>> array([0])
```

If you look at the data closely, you will notice that the information is not ordered although foo came before bar. This is because foo was encoded as two while bar was encoded as one. We will now use a different method of encoding the data in the data frame, especially if you need the data to be encoded in the right order. If you need to keep track of numerous categories, you may forget which strings you will need to map to integers. Therefore, we will create a dictionary that will make this process easier.

```
#Check mappings

list(l_encoder.classes_)

>> ['bar', 'baz', 'foo', 'x', 'y', 'z']

#Create dictionary of mappings

dict(zip(l_encoder.classes_,
l_encoder.transform(l_encoder.classes_)))

>> {'bar': 0, 'baz': 1, 'foo': 2, 'x': 3, 'y': 4, 'z': 5}
```

When you have a data frame, you will need to perform this function differently. That being said, it is easier to do this using a data frame. All you need to do is use the .apply() function, and apply the LabelEncoder to the data frame. When you do this, you will get a unique label for every value present in every column. If you look at the output, you will see that f00 is now encoded to one and so is the attribute y.

```
#Try LabelEncoder on a dataframe

import pandas as pd

l_encoder = preprocessing.LabelEncoder() #New object

df = pd.DataFrame(data = {'col1': ['foo','bar','foo','bar'],

                'col2': ['x', 'y', 'x', 'z'],

                'col3': [1, 2, 3, 4]})

#Now for the easy part

df.apply(l_encoder.fit_transform)

>>
```

|   | col1 | col2 | col3 |
|---|------|------|------|
| 0 | 1 | 0 | 0 |
| 1 | 0 | 1 | 1 |
| 2 | 1 | 0 | 2 |
| 3 | 0 | 2 | 3 |

We are now going to move onto encoding the categories ordinally. In this type of encoding, we will express the features in the form of integers. Each of these categories will have some structure and sense of place, in the sense that category x will come before category y. We are, however, going to include an additional condition. The values will not only be ordered, but they will also be paired with each other. Let us consider two arrays with the values ['foo', 'bar', 'baz'] and ['x', 'y', 'z']. We will now look at how we can encode the numbers zero, one, and two to every set of values between the two arrays. We can then encode one pair with a value. For example, ['foo', 'z'] would be mapped to [0, 2], and ['baz', 'x'] would be mapped to [2, 0].

It is a good idea to take this approach whenever you need to use a group of categories. This will make it easier for you to make these attributes available for regression.

```
from sklearn.preprocessing import OrdinalEncoder
o_encoder = OrdinalEncoder()
ary_2d = [['foo', 'bar', 'baz'], ['x', 'y', 'z']]
o_encoder.fit(2d_ary) #Fit the values
```

```
o_encoder.transform([['foo', 'y']])
```

```
>> array([[0., 1.]])
```

The classic dummy or one hot encoding is where you express every feature of categories in the data frame as an additional column of zeros and ones. This depends on the value that is present in the column. When you use this process, you can create a binary column for the category in the data frame. This will return a dense array or sparse matrix.

So, why do we use this? It is because this form of encoding is required when you want to feed the model in Scikit-learn with categorical data. Therefore, you should ensure that you are comfortable with this method.

```
from sklearn.preprocessing import OneHotEncoder

hot_encoder = OneHotEncoder(handle_unknown='ignore')

hot_encoder.fit(ary_2d)

hot_encoder.categories_

>>

[array(['foo', 'x'], dtype=object), array(['bar', 'y'], dtype=object),
array(['baz', 'z'], dtype=object)]

hot_encoder.transform([['foo', 'foo', 'baz'], ['y', 'y', 'x']]).toarray()

>>

array([[1., 0., 0., 0., 1., 0.],
       [0., 0., 0., 1., 0., 0.]])
```

So, what would we do if we were working with a data frame? Do you think we could still use one hot encoding? It is easier to use the data frame since all you will need to do is use the .get_dummies() function. This is included in the pandas library.

pd.get_dummies(df)=

| | col3 | col1_bar | col1_foo | col2_x | col2_y | col2_z |
|---|---|---|---|---|---|---|
| 0 | 1 | 0 | 1 | 1 | 0 | 0 |
| 1 | 2 | 1 | 0 | 0 | 1 | 0 |
| 2 | 3 | 0 | 1 | 1 | 0 | 0 |
| 3 | 4 | 1 | 0 | 0 | 0 | 1 |

In the above output, you will notice that two columns in the data frame have now been split. These have also been encoded to a binary framework in the data frame. For example, the column col1 in the data frame has been renamed to col1_bar, and now has the value one where term bar was the original value. You may also need to transform the features of the data frame within a specific limit or range. This can be done by using the MinMaxScaler function. Using this function you can scale every feature in the data frame. The default values are between zero and one, but you can change the range if required.

from sklearn.preprocessing import MinMaxScaler

mm_scaler = MinMaxScaler(feature_range=(0, 1)) #Between 0 and 1

mm_scaler.fit([ary_int])

```
>> MinMaxScaler(copy=True, feature_range=(0, 1))
print(scaler.data_max_)
>> [ 5. -41. -67. 23. -53. -57. -36. -25. 10. 17.]
print(mm_scaler.fit_transform([ary_int]))
>> [[0. 0. 0. 0. 0. 0. 0. 0. 0. 0.] #Humm something is wrong
```

If you look closely at the table, the numbers are all zero. This is not what we were trying to do. This may have happened for many reasons, but the primary reason is that the array being used in this example has not been formatted correctly. The array being used is of the dimension (1,n), but the dimension we need is (n,1). One of the easiest ways to manipulate the shape of an array is to ensure that it is a numpy array.

```
#Create numpy array
ary_int = np.array([ 5, -41, -67, 23, -53, -57, -36, -25, 10, 17])
#Transform
mm_scaler.fit_transform(ary_int[:, np.newaxis])
>>
array([[0.8        ],
       [0.28888889],
       [0.         ],
       [1.         ],
       [0.15555556],
       [0.11111111],
```

[0.34444444],

[0.46666667],

[0.85555556],

[0.93333333]])

#You can also use

mm_scaler.fit_transform(ary_int.reshape(-1, 1))

#Also try a different scale

mm_scaler = MinMaxScaler(feature_range=(0, 10))

mm_scaler.fit_transform(ary_int.reshape(-1, 1))

>>

array([[ 8.          ],

[ 2.88888889],

[ 0.     ],

[10.     ],

[ 1.55555556],

[ 1.11111111],

[ 3.44444444],

[ 4.66666667],

[ 8.55555556],

[ 9.33333333]])

You now finally know how to scale the data quickly using different sklearn packages. So, how do you give your data some sort of shape? I am talking about standardizing the data set so that you can create a gaussian distribution where the mean or average is zero and the standard deviation is one. You should always use this approach if you want to implement a gradient descent. You can also use this method when you are working with a regression model or developing a neural network. If you do want to implement a KNN, you should ensure that you scale the data. Remember that this approach is very different from normalization. To do this, you must use the function scale.

preprocessing.scale(foo)

>> array([ 0.86325871, -0.58600774, -1.40515833, 1.43036297, -0.96407724, -1.09010041, -0.42847877, -0.08191506, 1.02078767, 1.24132821])

preprocessing.scale(foo).mean()

>> -4.4408920985006264e-17 #Essentially zero

preprocessing.scale(foo).std()

>> 1.0 #Exactly what we wanted

Another package that you should look at in sklearn is Binarizer. You will only obtain zeros and ones as the output when you use this package, but you can define the terms. This process is used to threshold numerical values in the data set to obtain a Boolean output. The values that are greater than the threshold will be mapped to one while the values less than the threshold will be mapped to zero. This is a common process that is used in text mining or text preprocessing.

It is important for you to remember that you can use the functions transform() and fit() on a two-dimensional array alone. It is for this reason that we have nested one array within another in the above code. For instance, the threshold that we are using in this example is -25. This means that every number that is above -25 will be marked with the number 1.

```
from sklearn.preprocessing import Binarizer
#Set -25 as our threshold
tz = Binarizer(threshold=-25.0).fit([ary_int])
tz.transform([ary_int])
>>array([[1, 0, 0, 1, 0, 0, 0, 0, 1, 1]])
```

You have looked at numerous techniques in this chapter, and can now make an informed decision about which technique you can use for the algorithm you are using. It is a good idea to save a few intermediate databases that have binned or scaled data. This will help you view the effect of the output on the model that you develop. To summarize, it is important that you clean and prepare your data before you begin building your machine learning models.

# Chapter 6

# Packages Required for
# Machine Learning Applications

You will need to install numerous packages in your system before you work on building different machine learning algorithms. These packages are useful since they contain numerous functions and features that will make it easier to train the machine to solve a specific problem. You can also call on these functions when you are working on developing a machine learning model.

You should run the following command in a terminal:

pip install numpy

pip install scipy

pip install Scikit-learn

pip install matplotlib

pip install pandas

Write the code written below in Python to check the different versions of the library.

```
#Check the versions of libraries
#Python version
import sys
print('Python: {}'.format(sys.version))
#Scipy
import scipy
print('scipy: {}'.format(scipy.__version__))
#Numpy
import numpy
print('numpy: {}'.format(numpy.__version__))
#Matplotlib
import matplotlib
print('matplotlib: {}'.format(matplotlib.__version__))
#Pandas
import pandas
print('pandas: {}'.format(pandas.__version__))
#Scikit-learn
import sklearn
print('sklearn: {}'.format(sklearn.__version__))
```

The output will look as follows:

Python: 2.7.11 (default, Mar 1 2016, 18:40:10)

[GCC 4.2.1 Compatible Apple LLVM 7.0.2 (clang-700.1.81)] scipy: 0.17.0

numpy: 1.10.4

matplotlib: 1.5.1

pandas: 0.17.1

sklearn: 0.18.1

Now that you have the packages on your system, you should try to play around with some of the functions available so you know which ones you can use to build a machine learning model. For this, you should open a terminal and import the packages. You can access the documentation directly on the terminal.

## Libraries in Python

In this section, you will learn about the different libraries available in Python that you can use when you build a deep neural network. The list of libraries in this chapter is not exhaustive.

### *Keras*

Keras is a minimalist and modular neural network library that uses either Theano or TensorFlow as the backend. It allows the engineer to experiment with the data quickly and also ensures that the model predicts the results quickly. It is extremely easy to build a neural network on Keras since this library has numerous normalizers, optimizers, and activation functions.

Keras allows you to construct a sequence-based and graph-based network. This makes it easier for the engineer to implement complex architecture. The issue with Keras is that it never allows an engineer to train different models, networks, or layers in parallel. This is because it does not support the use of multiple GPUs.

## *Theano*

If Theano is not fully developed, it is difficult for engineers to identify or work on abstraction problems. Theano is a library that is often used to define, optimize, and evaluate numerous mathematical computations regardless of its complexity. This library is often used when the data set includes multi-dimensional arrays. This can be done by Theano since it helps the machine spread the work across multiple GPUs. This library can be integrated with numerous libraries in Python which enables an engineer to develop complex and better models.

## *TensorFlow*

TensorFlow is a package that has similar properties and functions like Theano. It is an open source package that is used to perform numerical computations. The Google Intelligence Organization developed this library, and an engineer can use the different functions and tools in this package to distribute the functions being performed by the model between different GPUs. TensorFlow is often used as the backend when you build a neural network in Python using Keras.

### *Scikit-learn*

Scikit-learn is an open source Python library. This library is often used to implement different visualization, machine learning, pre-processing, and cross-validation algorithms. This is often done using a unified interface. The functions and features in this package can be used for both data mining and data analysis. These functions include support vector machines, clustering, random forests, gradient boosting, classification, regression, and k-means algorithms.

# Chapter 7

# How to Clean Data Using Python

Most engineers and data scientists spend too much of their time cleaning a data set, and manipulating that data into a format that they can use to train the machines with. There are many data scientists who argue that the cleaning of data constitutes at least eighty percent of the job. Therefore, if you want to switch to this field, or if you are stepping into this field, you must learn how to deal with missing data, messy data, inconsistent formatting, outliers, and malformed records.

In this chapter, we will look at how to use the NumPy and Pandas libraries to clean the data sets. We will look at the following points:

- How to drop columns in a DataFrame.

- How to change the index in a DataFrame.

- How to clean the columns using .str().

- How to use the functioning DataFrame.applymap() to clean the complete data set.

- How to rename columns with recognizable labels.

- How to skip unnecessary rows.

In this chapter, we will be using the following data sets:

- BL-Flickr-Images-Book.csv – This is a .csv file which has information about the books in the British Library.

- university_towns.txt – This is a text file which contains information about the college towns in the US.

- olympics.csv – This is a .csv file which provides a summary of the countries that participated in the Summer and Winter Olympics.

These data sets can be downloaded from the GitHub repository for Python. Let us first import the NumPy and Pandas libraries to begin with the cleaning of data.

>>>

import pandas as pd

import numpy as np

## Dropping Columns in a Data Frame

You will see that you can use most categories of data in the data set for analysis. For instance, you are probably looking at a database that contains student information, including their personal information, but you only want to focus on the analysis of their grades. In this instance, the personal information is not necessary or important. You can remove these categories to reduce the amount of space that is taken up by the data set, thereby improving the performance of the program.

When you use Pandas, you can remove any unwanted row or column in a DataFrame using the drop() function. Let us now look at an example where we remove columns from a DataFrame. Before we do this, we must create a DataFrame of the BL-Flickr-Images-Book.csv file.

First, let's create a DataFrame out of the .csv file 'BL-Flickr-Images-Book.csv.' In the following example, we will be passing the path to pd.read.csv. This means that all the datasets from the .csv file are saved in the folder named "Datasets" in the current working directory.

```
>>>
df = pd.read_csv('Datasets/BL-Flickr-Images-Book.csv')
df.head()
Identifier Edition Statement Place of Publication \
0 206 NaN London
1 216 NaN London; Virtue & Yorston
2 218 NaN London
3 472 NaN London
4 480 A new edition, revised, etc. London
```

Date of Publication Publisher \

0 1879 [1878] S. Tinsley & Co.

1 1868 Virtue & Co.

2 1869 Bradbury, Evans & Co.

3 1851 James Darling

4 1857 Wertheim & Macintosh

Title Author \

0 Walter Forbes. [A novel.] By A. A A. A.

1 All for Greed. [A novel. The dedication signed... A., A. A.

2 Love the Avenger. By the author of "All for Gr... A., A. A.

3 Welsh Sketches, chiefly ecclesiastical, to the... A., E. S.

4 [The World in which I live, and my place in it... A., E. S.

Contributors Corporate Author \

0 FORBES, Walter. NaN

1 BLAZE DE BURY, Marie Pauline Rose - Baroness NaN

2 BLAZE DE BURY, Marie Pauline Rose - Baroness NaN

3 Appleyard, Ernest Silvanus. NaN

4 BROOME, John Henry. NaN

Corporate Contributors Former owner Engraver Issuance type \

0 NaN NaN NaN monographic

1 NaN NaN NaN monographic

2 NaN NaN NaN monographic

3 NaN NaN NaN monographic

4 NaN NaN NaN monographic

Flickr URL \

http://www.flickr.com/photos/britishlibrary/ta...

1 http://www.flickr.com/photos/britishlibrary/ta...

2 http://www.flickr.com/photos/britishlibrary/ta...

3 http://www.flickr.com/photos/britishlibrary/ta...

4 http://www.flickr.com/photos/britishlibrary/ta...

Shelfmarks

0 British Library HMNTS 12641.b.30.

1 British Library HMNTS 12626.cc.2.

2 British Library HMNTS 12625.dd.1.

3 British Library HMNTS 10369.bbb.15.

4 British Library HMNTS 9007.d.28.

We use the head() method to look at the first five entries. You will see that some of the columns provide some information about the various books which will help the library, but that information is not descriptive about the books: Edition Statement, Corporate Author, Corporate Contributors, Former owner, Engraver, Issuance type, and Shelfmarks.

To drop these columns, use the code below:

```
>>>

to_drop = ['Edition Statement',
... 'Corporate Author',
... 'Corporate Contributors',
... 'Former owner',
... 'Engraver',
... 'Contributors',
... 'Issuance type',
... 'Shelfmarks']
df.drop(to_drop, inplace=True, axis=1)
```

In the section above, we have listed the columns that we want to remove from the data set. For this, we will use the drop() function on the object, and pass the axis parameter as one and the inplace parameter as true. This will tell the Pandas directory that you want to change the object directly, and the directory should look for all the values in the column of that object that should be dropped.

When you look at the DataFrame now, you will see that the columns that we do not want to use have been removed.

```
>>>
>>> df.head()
```

Identifier Place of Publication Date of Publication \

0 206 London 1879 [1878]

1 216 London; Virtue & Yorston 1868

2 218 London 1869

3 472 London 1851

4 480 London 1857

Publisher Title \

S. Tinsley & Co. Walter Forbes. [A novel.] By A. A

1 Virtue & Co. All for Greed. [A novel. The dedication signed...

2 Bradbury, Evans & Co. Love the Avenger. By the author of "All for Gr...

3 James Darling Welsh Sketches, chiefly ecclesiastical, to the...

4 Wertheim & Macintosh [The World in which I live, and my place in it...

Author Flickr URL

0 A. A. http://www.flickr.com/photos/britishlibrary/ta...

1 A., A. A. http://www.flickr.com/photos/britishlibrary/ta...

2 A., A. A. http://www.flickr.com/photos/britishlibrary/ta...

3 A., E. S. http://www.flickr.com/photos/britishlibrary/ta...

4 A., E. S. http://www.flickr.com/photos/britishlibrary/ta...

You can also choose to remove the columns using the columns parameter instead of specifying which labels the directory needs to look at, and which axis should be considered.

```
>>>

>>> df.drop(columns=to_drop, inplace=True)
```

This is a more readable and intuitive syntax. It is apparent what we are doing here. If you know the columns that you want to retain, you can pass them through the argument usecols in the pd.read.csv function.

## Changing the Index of a Data Frame

The Index function in Pandas will allow you to extend the functionality of arrays in the NumPy directories. The function will also allow you to slice and label the data with ease. It is always a good idea to use a unique value to identify a field in the data set. For instance, you can expect that a librarian will always input the unique identifier for every book if he or she needs to search for the record.

```
>>>

df['Identifier'].is_unique

True
```

You can use the set_index method to replace the existing index using a column.

```
df = df.set_index('Identifier')

df.head()

Place of Publication Date of Publication \

206 London 1879 [1878]
```

216 London; Virtue & Yorston 1868

218 London 1869

472 London 1851

480 London 1857

Publisher \

206 S. Tinsley & Co.

216 Virtue & Co.

218 Bradbury, Evans & Co.

472 James Darling

480 Wertheim & Macintosh

Title Author \

206 Walter Forbes. [A novel.] By A. A A. A.

216 All for Greed. [A novel. The dedication signed... A., A. A.

218 Love the Avenger. By the author of "All for Gr... A., A. A.

472 Welsh Sketches, chiefly ecclesiastical, to the... A., E. S.

480 [The World in which I live, and my place in it... A., E. S.

Flickr URL

http://www.flickr.com/photos/britishlibrary/ta...

http://www.flickr.com/photos/britishlibrary/ta...

http://www.flickr.com/photos/britishlibrary/ta...

http://www.flickr.com/photos/britishlibrary/ta...

http://www.flickr.com/photos/britishlibrary/ta...

Every record in the DataFrame can be accessed using the loc[] function. This function will allow you to give every element in the cell an index based on the label. This means that you can give the record an index regardless of its position.

```
>>>

>>> df.loc[206]

Place of Publication London

Date of Publication 1879 [1878]

Publisher S. Tinsley & Co.

Title Walter Forbes. [A novel.] By A. A

Author A. A.

Flickr URL http://www.flickr.com/photos/britishlibrary/ta...

Name: 206, dtype: object
```

The number 206 is the first label for all the indices. If you want to access the label using its position, you can use df.iloc[0]. This function will give the element an index based on its position. .loc[] is a class instance, and it has a special syntax which does not follow the rules of a Python instance.

In the previous sections, the index being used was RangeIndex. This function labeled the elements with an index using integers, and this is analogous to the steps performed by the in-built function range. When you pass a column name to the set_index function, you will need to use the values in Identifier to change the index. If you looked closely, you would have noticed that we now use the object returned by the df = df.set_index(…) method as the variable. This is because this method does not make any changes directly to the object, but it does return a modified copy of that object. If you want to avoid this, you should schedule the inplace parameter.

df.set_index('Identifier', inplace=True)

## Tidying up Fields in the Data

We have now removed all the unnecessary columns in the DataFrame, and changed the indices to the DataFrame to something that is more sensible. This section will explain to you how you can only work on specific columns, and format them to help you get a better understanding. This will also help you enforce some consistency. We will be cleaning the fields 'Place of Publication' and 'Date of Publication.' When you inspect the data set further, you will notice that every data type is currently dtype. This object is similar to the str type in Python. This data type can encapsulate every field which cannot be labeled as categorical or numerical data. It makes sense to use this since we will be working with data sets that have a bunch of messy strings.

```
>>>

>>> df.get_dtype_counts()

objcct 6
```

You can enforce some numeric value to the date of publication field. This will allow you to perform other calculations down the road.

```
>>>

df.loc[1905:, 'Date of Publication'].head(10) Identifier

1905 1888

1929 1839, 38-54

2836 [1897?]

2854 1865

2956 1860-63

2957 1873

3017 1866

3131 1899

4598 1814

4884 1820
```

Name: Date of Publication, dtype: object

Every book can only have a single date of publication. Therefore, we will need to do the following:

- The extra dates in the square brackets need to be removed.

- The date ranges should always be converted to the "start date" wherever they are present.

- If we are uncertain about some dates, we will need to remove those dates and replace them with NaN from the NumPy directory.

- Convert the string nan to the NaN value.

You can take advantage of the regular expression by synthesizing these patterns. This will allow you to extract the year of publication.

>>>

regex = r'^(\d{4})'

You can find the four digits at the start of the string using the above regular expression. This is enough for us. The example used in the section above is a raw string. This means that the backslash used in this string cannot be used as an escape character. This is the standard practice when it comes to regular expressions. '(4)' in the above string will repeat the rule four times while '\d' represents a digit. The '^' depicts the start of the string, and the parentheses will denote the capturing group. This will signal to the Pandas directory that we only want to extract a portion of the regular expression. Let us now run this regular expression or regex across the DataFrame.

>>>

extr = df['Date of Publication'].str.extract(r'^(\d{4})', expand=False)

extr.head()

Identifier

1879

1868

1869

1851

1857

Name: Date of Publication, dtype: object

This column still has dtype, which is a string object. You can obtain the numerical version of that object using the pd.to.numeric function.

>>>

df['Date of Publication'] = pd.to_numeric(extr)

df['Date of Publication'].dtype dtype('float64')

This will show you that at least one value is missing from ten values. This should not worry you since you can now perform functions on all the valid values in the DataFrame.

>>>

df['Date of Publication'].isnull().sum() / len(df)
0.11717147339205986

This is now done.

## Combining NumPy and Str Methods to Clean Columns

In the above section, you will have noticed that the df['Date of Publication'].str is used to access some string operations in the Pandas directory. This attribute performs functions on compiled regular expressions or Python strings. If you want to clean the 'Place of Publication' field, you will need to combine the str method from the Pandas directories with the np.where function from the NumPy directories. This means that you will be creating a vectorized form of the if loop in Excel. The syntax is as follows:

```
>>>
```

```
>>> np.where(condition, then, else)
```

In the above section, the term condition can hold a Boolean mask or an array-like object. The then value is to be looked at if the condition is true, and the else section is looked at if the condition is false. The .where() method will take every cell or element, and check that element against the condition. If the value of the condition is True, the context in the condition will hold true, while the else condition is run if the condition is False. This can also be nested into a complex if-then statement, which will allow you to compute the values that are based on many conditions.

```
>>>
```

```
np.where(condition1, x1, np.where(condition2, x2,
np.where(condition3, x3, ...)))
```

Since the 'Place of Publication' column has only string values, we will be using these two functions to clean it. The contents of the column are given below:

```
>>>
```

```
df['Place of Publication'].head(10) Identifier
```

206 London

216 London; Virtue & Yorston

218 London

472 London

480 London

481 London

519 London

667 pp. 40. G. Bryan & Co: Oxford, 1898 London]

1143 London

Name: Place of Publication, dtype: object

You will notice that for some rows, there is some unnecessary information which surrounds the place of publication. If you look at the values closely, you will notice that this is only for some rows where the place of publication is 'Oxford' or 'London.' Let us now look at two different entries:

>>>

>>> df.loc[4157862]

Place of Publication Newcastle-upon-Tyne

Date of Publication 1867

Publisher T. Fordyce

Title Local Records; or, Historical Register of rema...

Author T. Fordyce

Flickr URL http://www.flickr.com/photos/britishlibrary/ta...

Name: 4157862, dtype: object

```
>>> df.loc[4159587]
```

Place of Publication Newcastle upon Tyne

Date of Publication 1834

Publisher Mackenzie & Dent

Title An historical, topographical and descriptive v...

Author E. (Eneas) Mackenzie

Flickr URL http://www.flickr.com/photos/britishlibrary/ta...

Name: 4159587, dtype: object

The books in the above list were published at the same time and in the same place, but there is one that has a hyphen while the other does not. You can use the str.contains() function to clean this column in one shot. Use the code below to clean these columns:

```
>>>
pub = df['Place of Publication']
london = pub.str.contains('London')
london[:5]
```

Identifier

True

True

True

True

True

Name: Place of Publication, dtype: bool

>>> oxford = pub.str.contains('Oxford')

These can be combined using the method np.where.

>>>

df['Place of Publication'] = np.where(london, 'London', np.where(oxford, 'Oxford',

pub.str.replace('-', ' ')))

df['Place of Publication'].head() Identifier

206 London

216 London

218 London

472 London

480 London

Name: Place of Publication, dtype: object

In the above example, the np.where() function is the nested structure. The condition in this structure is a series of Boolean values that are obtained using the function str.contains(). The contains() method allows Python to look for an entity in the substring of a string or an iterable. This method is similar to the keyword. The replacement that you will need to use is a string that will represent the place of publication. You can also replace a hyphen using a space. This can be done using the str.replace() function, and the column can be reassigned in the DataFrame. It is true that there is a lot more messy data in the DataFrame, but we will look at these columns for now. Let us now look at the first five rows in the DataFrame which looked better than they did when we started.

>>>

>>> df.head()

Place of Publication Date of Publication Publisher \

206 London 1879 S. Tinsley & Co.

216 London 1868 Virtue & Co.

218 London 1869 Bradbury, Evans & Co.

472 London 1851 James Darling

480 London 1857 Wertheim & Macintosh

Title Author \

206 Walter Forbes. [A novel.] By A. A AA

216 All for Greed. [A novel. The dedication signed... A. A A.

218 Love the Avenger. By the author of "All for Gr... A. A A.

472 Welsh Sketches, chiefly ecclesiastical, to the... E. S A.

480 [The World in which I live, and my place in it... E. S A.

Flickr URL

http://www.flickr.com/photos/britishlibrary/ta...

http://www.flickr.com/photos/britishlibrary/ta...

http://www.flickr.com/photos/britishlibrary/ta...

http://www.flickr.com/photos/britishlibrary/ta...

Cleaning the Entire Data Set Using the applymap()

In some instances, you will see that the "mess" is not only in one column, but can be found across the data set. You may need to apply a function to every cell or element in the data frame in some instances. You can use the applymap() function to apply one function to every cell or element in the DataFrame. This function is similar to the map() function. Let us look at the following example where we will create a DataFrame using the university_towns.txt file.

head Datasets/univerisity_towns.txt Alabama[edit]

Auburn (Auburn University)[1] Florence (University of North Alabama) Jacksonville (Jacksonville State University)[2] Livingston (University of West Alabama)[2] Montevallo (University of Montevallo)[2] Troy (Troy University)[2]

Tuscaloosa (University of Alabama, Stillman College, Shelton State)[3][4] Tuskegee (Tuskegee University)[5]

Alaska[edit]

In the above section, you will see that every periodic state name is followed by a university town in that state. For example, StateA TownA1 TownA2. If you look at how the names of the states are written, you will see that each one of them has the "[edit]" substring. You can create a list of tuples in the form (State, City), and wrap that list using a DataFrame.

```
>>>

university_towns = []

with open('Datasets/university_towns.txt') as file:

... for line in file:

... if '[edit]' in line:

... #Remember this `state` until the next is found

... state = line

... else:

... #Otherwise, we have a city; keep `state` as last-seen

... university_towns.append((state, line))

university_towns[:5]
```

[('Alabama[edit]\n', 'Auburn (Auburn University)[1]\n'), ('Alabama[edit]\n', 'Florence (University of North Alabama)\n'), ('Alabama[edit]\n', 'Jacksonville (Jacksonville State University)[2]\n'), ('Alabama[edit]\n', 'Livingston (University of West Alabama)[2]\n'), ('Alabama[edit]\n', 'Montevallo (University of Montevallo)[2]\n')]

This list can be wrapped using a DataFrame, and the columns can be set to "RegionName" and "State." The Pandas directory will consider every element in the above list and set the left value to State and the right value to RegionName. The DataFrame will now look like this:

```
>>>

towns_df = pd.DataFrame(university_towns,
```

... columns=['State', 'RegionName'])

towns_df.head()

State RegionName

0 Alabama[edit]\n Auburn (Auburn University)[1]\n

1 Alabama[edit]\n Florence (University of North Alabama)\n

2 Alabama[edit]\n Jacksonville (Jacksonville State University)[2]\n

3 Alabama[edit]\n Livingston (University of West Alabama)[2]\n

4 Alabama[edit]\n Montevallo (University of Montevallo)[2]\n

The strings could have been fixed or cleaned in the loop above. The Pandas directory will make it easier for you to do this. All you need is the name of the town and the state, and you can remove everything else. We can use the .str() method in this instance, but you can also use the applymap() method to map every element in the DataFrame to a Python callable. To understand what we mean by the term "element," you must look at the example given below:

>>>

1

Mock Data Set

1 Python Pandas

2 Real Python

3 NumPy Clean

In the above example, every cell is considered an element. Therefore, the applymap() function will look at each of these cells independently, and apply the necessary function. Let us now define that function:

>>>

```
def get_citystate(item):
... if ' (' in item:
... return item[:item.find(' (')]
... elif '[' in item:
... return item[:item.find('[')]
... else:
... return item
```

The applymap() function in the Pandas directory only takes one parameter. This parameter is the function, also called the callable, which can be applied to every element.

>>>

```
>>> towns_df = towns_df.applymap(get_citystate)
```

We will first need to define a function in Python which will pick an element as a parameter from the DataFrame. A check will then be performed within the function to determine whether the element contains a "(" or "[" or not. Based on the value of the check, the values are mapped to that element by the function. The applymap() function will then be called on the object. If you look at the DataFrame now, you will see that it is neater than before.

```
>>>

towns_df.head() State RegionName

0 Alabama Auburn

1 Alabama Florence

2 Alabama Jacksonville

3 Alabama Livingston

4 Alabama Montevallo
```

In the above section of the code, the applymap() method looked at every element in the DataFrame, and passed that element to the function after which the returned value was used to replace the original value. It is this simple. The applymap() method is both a convenient and versatile method. This method can, however, take some time to run for large data sets. This is because it maps every individual element to a Python callable. Therefore, it is always a good idea to use vectorized operations that use the NumPy or Cython directories.

## Renaming Columns and Skipping Rows

There are times when you will have datasets that have some unnecessary or unimportant information in the first or last rows or column names that are difficult to understand. For instance, there can be some definitions or footnotes in the data set which are not necessary for you to use. In this case, you should skip those rows or rename the columns, so you can remove the unnecessary information or work with sensible labels. Let us first look at the first few rows in the Olympics.csv data set before we look at how this can be done.

```
head -n 5 Datasets/olympics.csv
0,1,2,3,4,5,6,7,8,9,10,11,12,13,14,15
```

,? Summer,01 !,02 !,03 !,Total,? Winter,01 !,02 !,03 !,Total,? Games,01 !,02 !,03 !,Combined total Afghanistan (AFG),13,0,0,2,2,0,0,0,0,0,13,0,0,2,2

Algeria (ALG),12,5,2,8,15,3,0,0,0,0,15,5,2,8,15

Argentina (ARG),23,18,24,28,70,18,0,0,0,0,41,18,24,28,70
Now, we'll read it into a Pandas DataFrame:

```
>>>

>>> olympics_df = pd.read_csv('Datasets/olympics.csv')

>>> olympics_df.head()
```

0 1 2 3 4 5 6 7 8 \

0 NaN ? Summer 01 ! 02 ! 03 ! Total ? Winter 01 ! 02 ! 1 Afghanistan (AFG) 13 0 0 2 2 0 0 0

2 Algeria (ALG) 12 5 2 8 15 3 0 0

3 Argentina (ARG) 23 18 24 28 70 18 0 0 4 Armenia (ARM) 5 1 2 9 12 6 0 0

9 10 11 12 13 14 15

0 03 ! Total ? Games 01 ! 02 ! 03 ! Combined total

1 0 0 13 0 0 2 2

2 0 0 15 5 2 8 15

3 0 0 41 18 24 28 70

4 0 0 11 1 2 9 12

This is certainly messy. Every column is indexed at zero, and is the string form of the integer. The row that you are using to set the names of the other columns is at the Olympics_df.iloc[0]. This is because the file that we are using starts the indexing at 0 and ends at 15.

If you want to go to the source of the data set, you will see that NaN above a column will represent Country, "? Summer" will represent the Summer Games, "01!" represents Gold, etc. Therefore, we will need to do the following:

Skip the first row and set the index as zero and for the headers rename all the columns.

You can pass some parameters in the read.csv() function if you want to skip some rows and set the index for the headers as one. The function read.csv does use a lot of parameters, but in this instance, we only need to remove the first row (which has the index zero).

>>>  olympics_df  =  pd.read_csv('Datasets/olympics.csv', header=1)

olympics_df.head()

Unnamed: 0 ? Summer 01 ! 02 ! 03 ! Total ? Winter \ 0 Afghanistan (AFG) 13 0 0 2 2 0 1 Algeria (ALG) 12 5 2 8 15 3

2 Argentina (ARG) 23 18 24 28 70 18

3 Armenia (ARM) 5 1 2 9 12 6

4 Australasia (ANZ) [ANZ] 2 3 4 5 12 0

01 !.1 02 !.1 03 !.1 Total.1 ? Games 01 !.2 02 !.2 03 !.2 \

0 0 0 0 0 13 0 0 2

1 0 0 0 0 15 5 2 8

2 0 0 0 0 41 18 24 28

3 0 0 0 0 11 1 2 9

4 0 0 0 0 2 3 4 5

Combined total

2

1 15

2 70

3 12

4 12

The data set no longer has any unnecessary rows, and the correct names have been used for all fields. You should see how the Pandas library has changed the name of the Countries column from NaN to Unnamed: 0.

To rename the columns, we will use the rename() method in the DataFrame. This will allow you to re-label any axis in the data set using a mapping function. In this instance, we will need to use dict. We must first define the dictionary which will map the existing names of the columns to the usable names which are present in the dictionary.

>>>

new_names = {'Unnamed: 0': 'Country',

... '? Summer': 'Summer Olympics',

... '01 !': 'Gold',

... '02 !': 'Silver',

... '03 !': 'Bronze',

... '? Winter': 'Winter Olympics',

... '01 !.1': 'Gold.1',

... '02 !.1': 'Silver.1',

... '03 !.1': 'Bronze.1',

... '? Games': '#Games',

... '01 !.2': 'Gold.2',

... '02 !.2': 'Silver.2',

... '03 !.2': 'Bronze.2'}

We will now call upon the rename() function on the object.

>>>

>>> olympics_df.rename(columns=new_names, inplace=True)

If you want changes to be made directly to the object, you should set inplace to True. Let us see if this works for us:

```
>>>

>>> olympics_df.head()

Country Summer Olympics Gold Silver Bronze Total \
0 Afghanistan (AFG) 13 0 0 2 2
1 Algeria (ALG) 12 5 2 8 15
2 Argentina (ARG) 23 18 24 28 70
3 Armenia (ARM) 5 1 2 9 12
4 Australasia (ANZ) [ANZ] 2 3 4 5 12

Winter Olympics Gold.1 Silver.1 Bronze.1 Total.1 #Games
Gold.2 \
0 0 0 0 0 0 0 13 0
1 3 0 0 0 0 15 5
2 18 0 0 0 0 41 18
3 6 0 0 0 0 11 1
4 0 0 0 0 0 2 3

Silver.2 Bronze.2 Combined total
0 0 2 2
1 2 8 15
2 24 28 70
3 2 9 12
4 4 5 12
```

## Python Data Cleaning: Recap and Resources

In this chapter, you gathered information on how you can remove any unnecessary fields in a data set, and how you can set an index for every field in the data set to make it easier for you to access that field. You also learned how you can use the applymap() function to clean the complete data set, and to use the .str() accessor to clean specific object fields. It is important to know how to clean data since it is a big part of data analytics. You now know how you can use NumPy and Pandas to clean different data sets.

# Chapter 8

# Manipulation Of Data In Python

In this chapter we will look at how we can use the NumPy and Pandas libraries to manipulate data in a data set.

## NumPy

#Load the library and check its version, just to make sure we aren't using an older version

import numpy as np

np.__version__

'1.12.1'

#Create a list comprising numbers from 0 to 9

L = list(range(10))

#Converting integers to string - this style of handling lists is known as list comprehension.

#List comprehension offers in a versatile way to handle list manipulations tasks easily.

We'll learn about them in future tutorials. Here's an example.

```
[str(c) for c in L]
['0', '1', '2', '3', '4', '5', '6', '7', '8', '9']
[type(item) for item in L]
[int, int, int, int, int, int, int, int, int, int]
```

### *Creating Arrays*

An array is a homogeneous data type, in the sense that it can only hold variables of the same data type. This holds true for arrays in NumPy as well.

```
#Creating arrays
np.zeros(10, dtype='int')
array([0, 0, 0, 0, 0, 0, 0, 0, 0, 0])
#Creating a 3 row x 5 column matrix
np.ones((3,5), dtype=float)
array([[ 1., 1., 1., 1., 1.],
1., 1., 1., 1., 1.],
1., 1., 1., 1., 1.]])
#Creating a matrix with a predefined value np.full((3,5),1.23)
array([[ 1.23, 1.23, 1.23, 1.23, 1.23],
1.23, 1.23, 1.23, 1.23, 1.23],
1.23, 1.23, 1.23, 1.23, 1.23]])
#Create an array with a set sequence np.arange(0, 20, 2)
```

array([0, 2, 4, 6, 8,10,12,14,16,18])

#Create an array of even space between the given range of values np.linspace(0, 1, 5)

array([ 0., 0.25, 0.5 , 0.75, 1.])

#Create a 3x3 array with mean 0 and standard deviation 1 in a given dimension np.random.normal(0, 1, (3,3))

array([[ 0.72432142, -0.90024075, 0.27363808],

0.88426129, 1.45096856, -1.03547109], [-0.42930994, -1.02284441, -1.59753603]]) #Create an identity matrix

np.eye(3) array([[ 1., 0., 0.],

0., 1., 0.],

0., 0., 1.]])

#Set a random seed np.random.seed(0)

x1 = np.random.randint(10, size=6) #One dimension

x2 = np.random.randint(10, size=(3,4)) #Two dimension

x3 = np.random.randint(10, size=(3,4,5)) #Three dimension

print("x3 ndim:", x3.ndim)

print("x3 shape:", x3.shape)

print("x3 size: ", x3.size)

('x3 ndim:', 3)

('x3 shape:', (3, 4, 5))

('x3 size: ', 60)

## Array Indexing

If you are familiar with programming languages, you will be aware that the indexing in an array always begins at zero.

```
x1 = np.array([4, 3, 4, 4, 8, 4])

x1

array([4, 3, 4, 4, 8, 4])

#Assess value to index zero

x1[0]

4

#Assess fifth value

x1[4]

8

#Get the last value

x1[-1]

4

#Get the second last value

x1[-2]

8
```

#In a multidimensional array, we need to specify row and column index x2

```
array([[3, 7, 5, 5],

[0, 1, 5, 9],
```

[3, 0, 5, 0]])

#1st row and 2nd column value

x2[2,3]

0

#3rd row and last value from the 3rd column

x2[2,-1]

0

#Replace value at 0,0 index

x2[0,0] = 12

x2

array([[12, 7, 5, 5],

0, 1, 5, 9],

3, 0, 5, 0]])

## Array Slicing

You can slice an array to access a specific element or a range of elements within an array.

x = np.arange(10)

x

array([0, 1, 2, 3, 4, 5, 6, 7, 8, 9])

#From start to 4th position

x[:5]

```
array([0, 1, 2, 3, 4])
```

#From 4th position to end

```
x[4:]
array([4, 5, 6, 7, 8, 9])
```

#From 4th to 6th position

```
x[4:7]
array([4, 5, 6])
```

#Return elements at even place

```
x[ : : 2]
array([0, 2, 4, 6, 8])
```

#Return elements from first position step by two

```
x[1::2]
array([1, 3, 5, 7, 9])
```

#Reverse the array

```
x[::-1]
array([9, 8, 7, 6, 5, 4, 3, 2, 1, 0])
```

### *Array Concatenation*

It helps to combine multiple arrays to perform complex operations. You will not have to type the elements in the different arrays, but can instead concatenate those arrays to handle these complex operations with ease.

#You can concatenate two or more arrays at once.

```python
x = np.array([1, 2, 3])

y = np.array([3, 2, 1])

z = [21,21,21]

np.concatenate([x, y,z])

array([ 1, 2, 3, 3, 2, 1, 21, 21, 21])

#You can also use this function to create 2-dimensional arrays.

grid = np.array([[1,2,3],[4,5,6]])

np.concatenate([grid,grid])

array([[1, 2, 3],

[4, 5, 6],

[1, 2, 3],

[4, 5, 6]])

#Using its axis parameter, you can define row-wise or column-
wise matrix np.concatenate([grid,grid],axis=1)

array([[1, 2, 3, 1, 2, 3],

[4, 5, 6, 4, 5, 6]])
```

In the above code, we have used the concatenation function on those arrays that have variables of the same data type and the same dimensions. So, what if you need to combine a one-dimensional array with a two-dimensional array? You can use the np.vstack or the np.hstack functions in such instances. The next section of code will help you understand how this can be done.

x = np.array([3,4,5])

grid = np.array([[1,2,3],[17,18,19]])

np.vstack([x,grid])

array([[ 3, 4, 5],

1, 2, 3], [17, 18, 19]])

#Similarly, you can add an array using np.hstack z = np.array([[9],[9]])

np.hstack([grid,z]) array([[ 1, 2, 3, 9], [17, 18, 19, 9]])

It is always a good idea to use a predefined position or condition to split an array.

x = np.arange(10)

x

array([0, 1, 2, 3, 4, 5, 6, 7, 8, 9]) x1,x2,x3 = np.split(x,[3,6]) print x1,x2,x3

[0 1 2] [3 4 5] [6 7 8 9]

grid = np.arange(16).reshape((4,4)) grid

upper,lower = np.vsplit(grid,[2]) print (upper, lower)

(array([[0, 1, 2, 3],

[4, 5, 6, 7]]), array([[ 8, 9, 10, 11], [12, 13, 14, 15]]))

The NumPy directory gives you access to numerous mathematical functions apart from the functions that have been used in the examples above. Some of these functions include sum, divide, abs, multiple, mod, power, log, sin, tan, cos, mean, min, max, var, etc.

You can use these functions to perform numerous arithmetic calculations. To learn more about these functions, you should refer to the NumPy documentation to learn more about the functions. Let us now take a look at how you can manipulate data using the Pandas library. Ensure that you look at every line in the code carefully before you manipulate the data.

## Let's start with Pandas

#Load library - pd is just an alias. I used pd because it's short and literally abbreviates pandas.

#You can use any name as an alias.

import pandas as pd

#Create a DataFrame - dictionary is used here where keys get converted to column names and values to row values.

```
data = pd.DataFrame({'Country':
['Russia','Colombia','Chile','Equador','Nigeria'],
Rank':[121,40,100,130,11]})
data
CountryRank
0Russia121
1Colombia40
2Chile100
3Equador130
```

4Nigeria11

#We can do a quick analysis of any data set using:

data.describe()

Rank

count5.000000

mean80.400000

std52.300096

min11.000000

25%40.000000

50%100.000000

75%121.000000

max130.000000

You can obtain the summary of the statistics of only the integer and double variables using the describe() method. If you want to obtain all the information available about the data set, you should use the function named info().

#Among other things, it shows the data set has 5 rows and 2 columns with their respective names. data.info()

<class 'pandas.core.frame.DataFrame'>

RangeIndex: 5 entries, 0 to 4

Data columns (total 2 columns):

Country 5 non-null object

Rank 5 non-null int64

dtypes: int64(1), object(1)

memory usage: 152.0+ bytes

#Let's create another data frame

data = pd.DataFrame({'group':['a', 'a', 'a', 'b','b', 'b', 'c', 'c','c'],'ounces':[4, 3, 12, 6, 7.5, 8, 3, 5, 6]})

data

groupounces

0a4.0

1a3.0

2a12.0

3b6.0

4b7.5

5b8.0

6c3.0

7c5.0

8c6.0

#Let's sort the data frame by ounces - inplace = True will make changes to the data
data.sort_values(by=['ounces'],ascending=True,inplace=False)
groupounces

1a3.0

6c3.0

0a4.0

7c5.0

3b6.0

8c6.0

4b7.5

5b8.0

2a12.0

The data can now be sorted using numerous columns.

data.sort_values(by=['group','ounces'],ascending=[True,False],i
nplace=False)

groupounces

2a12.0

0a4.0

1a3.0

5b8.0

4b7.5

3b6.0

8c6.0

7c5.0

6c3.0

Most data sets have duplicate rows and columns, and these duplicate rows are called noise. It is for this reason that you should always remove all the inconsistencies in the data set before you feed the model with the data set. Let us look at an alternative way to remove the duplicates in the data set.

#Create another data with duplicate rows

data = pd.DataFrame({'k1':['one']*3 + ['two']*4, 'k2':[3,2,1,3,3,4,4]})

data

k1k2

0one3

1one2

2one1

3two3

4two3

5two4

6two4

#Sort values

data.sort_values(by='k2')

k1k2

2one1

1one2

0one3

3two3

4two3

5two4

6two4

```
#Remove duplicates - ta da!
data.drop_duplicates()
```

k1k2

0one3

1one2

2one1

3two3

5two4

In the example above, the values present in the rows and columns have been matched to remove the duplicates in the data set. The duplicates can also be removed using specific columns as parameters. Let us look at how the duplicates in Column K can be removed.

```
data.drop_duplicates(subset='k1')
```

k1k2

0one3

3two3

Let us now understand how the data can be categorized based on some predefined rules or criteria. This will often happen when you work on processing data, especially that data which needs to be categorized. For example, if you have a column with the names of countries in it, and you want to split the countries into separate columns based on their continents. To do this you will need to create a new variable. The code below will help you achieve this with ease.

```
data = pd.DataFrame({'food': ['bacon', 'pulled pork', 'bacon',
    'Pastrami','corned    beef',   'Bacon',   'pastrami',   'honey
    ham','nova lox'],

'ounces': [4, 3, 12, 6, 7.5, 8, 3, 5, 6]})

data

foodounces

0bacon4.0

1pulled pork3.0

2bacon12.0

3Pastrami6.0

4corned beef7.5

5Bacon8.0

6pastrami3.0

7honey ham5.0

8nova lox6.0
```

Let us now look at how we can create a new variable that will help the model predict which animal will be the source of food for another animal. For the model to do this, we should first map the food to the animals by using the dictionary. The map function can then be used to pull the values in from the dictionary. The code below will help us achieve this.

```
meat_to_animal = {
'bacon': 'pig',
'pulled pork': 'pig',
'pastrami': 'cow',
'corned beef': 'cow',
'honey ham': 'pig',
'nova lox': 'salmon'
}
def meat_2_animal(series):
if series['food'] == 'bacon':
return 'pig'
elif series['food'] == 'pulled pork':
return 'pig'
elif series['food'] == 'pastrami':
return 'cow'
elif series['food'] == 'corned beef':
return 'cow'
elif series['food'] == 'honey ham':
return 'pig'
```

```python
    else:
        return 'salmon'
#Create a new variable
data['animal']                                    =
    data['food'].map(str.lower).map(meat_to_animal)
data
```

foodouncesanimal

0bacon4.0pig

1pulled pork3.0pig

2bacon12.0pig

3Pastrami6.0cow

4corned beef7.5cow

5Bacon8.0pig

6pastrami3.0cow

7honey ham5.0pig

8nova lox6.0salmon

```python
#Another way of doing it is: convert the food values to the
    lower case and apply the function
lower = lambda x: x.lower()
data['food'] = data['food'].apply(lower)
data['animal2'] = data.apply(meat_2_animal, axis='columns')
data
```

foodouncesanimalanimal2

0bacon4.0pigpig

1pulled pork3.0pigpig

2bacon12.0pigpig

3pastrami6.0cowcow

4corned beef7.5cowcow

5bacon8.0pigpig

6pastrami3.0cowcow

7honey ham5.0pigpig

8nova lox6.0salmonsalmon

Alternatively, you can use the assign function if you wish to create another variable. You will come across numerous functions in this chapter that you should keep in mind. This section will help you understand how you can use the Pandas library to solve different machine learning problems.

data.assign(new_variable = data['ounces']*10)

foodouncesanimalanimal2new_variable

0bacon4.0pigpig40.0

1pulled pork3.0pigpig30.0

2bacon12.0pigpig120.0

3pastrami6.0cowcow60.0

4corned beef7.5cowcow75.0

5bacon8.0pigpig80.0

6pastrami3.0cowcow30.0

7honey ham5.0pigpig50.0

8nova lox6.0salmonsalmon60.0

Let us now remove the animal2 column from the dataframe.

data.drop('animal2',axis='columns',inplace=True)

data

foodouncesanimal

0bacon4.0pig

1pulled pork3.0pig

2bacon12.0pig

3Pastrami6.0cow

4corned beef7.5cow

5Bacon8.0pig

6pastrami3.0cow

7honey ham5.0pig

8nova lox6.0salmon

When you load a data set from the Internet, it is possible that there will be some missing variables in the set. You can either substitute the missing variable with a dummy variable or a default value depending on the type of problem you are solving. It can also be that there are many outliers in the data set that you want to get rid of. Let us look at how this can be done using the Pandas directory.

```
#Series function from pandas are used to create arrays

data = pd.Series([1., -999., 2., -999., -1000., 3.])

data

0 1.0

-999.0

2 2.0

3 -999.0

4 -1000.0

5 3.0

dtype: float64

#Replace    -999    with    NaN    values    data.replace(-999,
    np.nan,inplace=True) data

0 1.0

NaN

2.0

3 NaN

4 -1000.0

5 3.0

dtype: float64
```

#We can also replace multiple values at once. data = pd.Series([1., -999., 2., -999., -1000., 3.]) data.replace([-999,-1000],np.nan,inplace=True) data

0 1.0

1 NaN

2.0

NaN

4 NaN

5 3.0

dtype: float64

Let us now look at how we can rename the rows and columns.

data = pd.DataFrame(np.arange(12).reshape((3, 4)),index=['Ohio', 'Colorado', 'New York'],columns=['one', 'two', 'three', 'four'])

data

onetwothreefour

Ohio0123

Colorado4567

New York891011

Using rename function

data.rename(index = {'Ohio':'SanF'}, columns={'one':'one_p','two':'two_p'},inplace=True) data

one_ptwo_pthreefour

SanF0123

Colorado4567

New York891011

```
#You can also use string functions
data.rename(index = str.upper, columns=str.title,inplace=True)
data
```

One_pTwo_pThreeFour

SANF0123

COLORADO4567

NEW YORK891011

We will need to split or categorize the continuous variables.

```
ages = [20, 22, 25, 27, 21, 23, 37, 31, 61, 45, 41, 32]
```

Let us now divide the ages into smaller segments or bins like 18-25, 26-35, 36-60, and 60 and above.

```
#Understand the output - '(' means the value is included in the
bin, '[' means the value is excluded
bins = [18, 25, 35, 60, 100]
cats = pd.cut(ages, bins)
cats
```

[(18, 25], (18, 25], (18, 25], (25, 35], (18, 25], ..., (25, 35], (60, 100], (35, 60], (35, 60], (25, 35]] Length: 12

Categories (4, object): [(18, 25] < (25, 35] < (35, 60] < (60, 100]] #To include the right bin value, we can do: pd.cut(ages,bins,right=False)

[[18, 25), [18, 25), [25, 35), [25, 35), [18, 25), ..., [25, 35), [60, 100), [35, 60), [35, 60), [25, 35)] Length: 12

Categories (4, object): [[18, 25) < [25, 35) < [35, 60) < [60, 100)] #Pandas library intrinsically assigns an encoding to categorical variables. cats.labels

array([0, 0, 0, 1, 0, 0, 2, 1, 3, 2, 2, 1], dtype=int8)

#Let's check how many observations fall under each bin

pd.value_counts(cats)

(18, 25] 5

(35, 60] 3

(25, 35] 3

(60, 100] 1

dtype: int64

We can also pass a name to every label.

bin_names = ['Youth', 'YoungAdult', 'MiddleAge', 'Senior']
new_cats = pd.cut(ages, bins,labels=bin_names)

pd.value_counts(new_cats)

Youth5

MiddleAge3

YoungAdult3

Senior1

dtype: int64

#We can also calculate their cumulative sum

pd.value_counts(new_cats).cumsum()

Youth5

MiddleAge3

YoungAdult3

Senior1

dtype: int64

You can also create pivots and group different variables in the data set using the Pandas directories. A pivot table is one of the easiest ways to perform an analysis of the data set, and it is for this reason that it is essential that you understand how this can be done.

```
df = pd.DataFrame({'key1' : ['a', 'a', 'b', 'b', 'a'],

'key2' : ['one', 'two', 'one', 'two', 'one'],

'data1' : np.random.randn(5),

'data2' : np.random.randn(5)})

df
```

data1data2key1key2

00.9735990.001761a

10.207283-0.990160a

21.0996421.872394b

30.939897-0.241074b

40.6063890.053345a

#Calculate the mean of data1 column by key1

grouped = df['data1'].groupby(df['key1'])

grouped.mean()

key1

0.595757 b 1.019769

Name: data1, dtype: float64

#We will now slice the data frame

dates = pd.date_range('20130101',periods=6)

df                                                                =
pd.DataFrame(np.random.randn(6,4),index=dates,columns=list(
'ABCD')) df

ABCD

2013-01-011.030816-1.2769890.837720-1.490111 2013-01-02-
1.070215-0.2091290.604572-1.743058

2013-01-031.5242271.8635751.2913781.300696

2013-01-040.918203-0.158800-0.964063-1.990779

2013-01-050.0897310.114854-0.5858150.298772

2013-01-060.2222600.435183-0.0457480.049898 #Get first n
rows from the data frame df[:3]

ABCD

2013-01-011.030816-1.2769890.837720-1.490111

2013-01-02-1.070215-0.2091290.604572-1.743058

2013-01-031.5242271.8635751.2913781.300696

#Slice based on date range

df['20130101':'20130104']

ABCD

2013-01-011.030816-1.2769890.837720-1.490111

2013-01-02-1.070215-0.2091290.604572-1.743058

2013-01-031.5242271.8635751.2913781.300696

2013-01-040.918203-0.158800-0.964063-1.990779     #Slicing based on column names df.loc[:,['A','B']]

AB

2013-01-011.030816-1.276989

2013-01-02-1.070215-0.209129

2013-01-031.5242271.863575

2013-01-040.918203-0.158800

2013-01-050.0897310.114854

2013-01-060.2222600.435183

#Slicing based on both row index labels and column names df.loc['20130102':'20130103',['A','B']] AB

2013-01-02-1.070215-0.209129

2013-01-031.5242271.863575

#Slicing based on index of columns

```
df.iloc[3] #Returns 4th row (index is 3rd)
```

0.918203 B -0.158800 C -0.964063 D -1.990779

```
Name: 2013-01-04 00:00:00, dtype: float64 #Returns a specific
range of rows df.iloc[2:4, 0:2]
```

AB

2013-01-031.5242271.863575

2013-01-040.918203-0.158800

```
#Returns specific rows and columns using lists containing
columns or row indexes
df.iloc[[1,5],[0,2]]
```

AC

2013-01-02-1.0702150.604572

2013-01-060.222260-0.045748

You can also perform Boolean indexing using the values in the columns. This will help you filter the data set based on some conditions. These conditions must be pre-defined.

```
df[df.A > 1]
```

ABCD

2013-01-011.030816-1.2769890.837720-1.490111

2013-01-031.5242271.8635751.2913781.300696

```
#We can copy the data set
df2 = df.copy()
```

```python
df2['E']=['one', 'one','two','three','four','three']
df2
```

ABCDE

2013-01-011.030816-1.2769890.837720-1.490111one

2013-01-02-1.070215-0.2091290.604572-1.743058one

2013-01-031.5242271.8635751.2913781.300696two

2013-01-040.918203-0.158800-0.964063-1.990779three

2013-01-050.0897310.114854-0.5858150.298772four

2013-01-060.2222600.435183-0.0457480.049898three   #Select rows based on column values df2[df2['E'].isin(['two','four'])] ABCDE

2013-01-031.5242271.8635751.2913781.300696two

2013-01-050.0897310.114854-0.5858150.298772four   #Select all rows except those with two and four df2[~df2['E'].isin(['two','four'])] ABCDE

2013-01-011.030816-1.2769890.837720-1.490111one

2013-01-02-1.070215-0.2091290.604572-1.743058one

2013-01-040.918203-0.158800-0.964063-1.990779three

2013-01-060.2222600.435183-0.0457480.049898three

You can also select columns using a query method. In this method, you will need to enter a criterion.

```python
#List all columns where A is greater than C
df.query('A > C')
```

```
                 A         B         C         D
2013-01-01  1.030816 -1.276989  0.837720 -1.490111
2013-01-03  1.524227  1.863575  1.291378  1.300696
2013-01-04  0.918203 -0.158800 -0.964063 -1.990779
2013-01-05  0.089731  0.114854 -0.585815  0.298772
2013-01-06  0.222260  0.435183 -0.045748  0.049898
```
#Using OR condition

df.query('A < B | C > A')

```
                 A         B         C         D
2013-01-02 -1.070215 -0.209129  0.604572 -1.743058
2013-01-03  1.524227  1.863575  1.291378  1.300696
2013-01-05  0.089731  0.114854 -0.585815  0.298772
2013-01-06  0.222260  0.435183 -0.045748  0.049898
```

A pivot table allows you to customize the format of the information to help you understand the data set better. Most people use Excel to build a pivot table since that helps them understand and analyze the data fairly easily.

```
#Create a data frame
data = pd.DataFrame({'group': ['a', 'a', 'a', 'b','b', 'b', 'c', 'c','c'],
'ounces': [4, 3, 12, 6, 7.5, 8, 3, 5, 6]})
data
```
group ounces

0a4.0

1a3.0

2a12.0

3b6.0

4b7.5

5b8.0

6c3.0

7c5.0

8c6.0

#Calculate means of each group

data.pivot_table(values='ounces',index='group',aggfunc=np.mean)

group

6.333333 b 7.166667 c 4.666667

Name: ounces, dtype: float64 #Calculate count by each group

data.pivot_table(values='ounces',index='group',aggfunc='count')
group

3

3 c 3

Name: ounces, dtype: int64

Now that we are familiar with both the NumPy and Pandas libraries, let us look at a real-world example and see how the functions that we have learned in the previous sections will help us explore the data set.

## Exploring The Data Set

We are going to work with a data set with information about adults in this section. This data set has been taken from the UCI Machine Learning Repository, and can be downloaded from the following location:

https://s3-ap-southeast-1.amazonaws.com/he-public-data/datafiles19cdaf8.zip

The data set poses a binary classification problem, and the objective is to calculate the salary of an individual using some variables.

```
#Load the data

train = pd.read_csv("~/Adult/train.csv")

test = pd.read_csv("~/Adult/test.csv")

#Check data set

train.info()

<class 'pandas.core.frame.DataFrame'>

RangeIndex: 32561 entries, 0 to 32560

Data columns (total 15 columns):

age 32561 non-null int64

workclass 30725 non-null object

fnlwgt 32561 non-null int64
```

education 32561 non-null object

education.num 32561 non-null int64

marital.status 32561 non-null object

occupation 30718 non-null object

relationship 32561 non-null object

race 32561 non-null object

sex 32561 non-null object

capital.gain 32561 non-null int64

capital.loss 32561 non-null int64

hours.per.week 32561 non-null int64

native.country 31978 non-null object

target 32561 non-null object

dtypes: int64(6), object(9)

memory usage: 3.7+ MB

The training data set that we are using for this example has 32561 rows and 15 columns. Out of these fifteen columns, only six columns have integer data, while the other columns have object or character data. You can also check the test data set in a similar manner. The number of rows and columns in the data set can also be identified using the following code:

```
print ("The train data has",train.shape)
print ("The test data has",test.shape)
```

('The train data has', (32561, 15))

('The test data has', (16281, 15))

#Let's have a glimpse of the data set

train.head()

ageworkclassfnlwgteducationeducation.nummarital.statusoccup ationrelationshipracesexcapital.gaincapit

al.losshours.per.weeknative.countrytarget

039State-gov77516Bachelors13Never-marriedAdm-clericalNot-in-familyWhiteMale2174040United-States<=50K

150Self-emp-not-inc83311Bachelors13Married-civ-spouseExec-managerialHusbandWhiteMale0013United-States<=50K

238Private215646HS-grad9DivorcedHandlers-cleanersNot-in-familyWhiteMale0040United-States<=50K

353Private23472111th7Married-civ-spouseHandlers-cleanersHusbandBlackMale0040United-States<=50K

428Private338409Bachelors13Married-civ-spouseProf-specialtyWifeBlackFemale0040Cuba<=50K Let us verify if the data set has any missing values. nans = train.shape[0] - train.dropna().shape[0]

print ("%d rows have missing values in the train data" %nans)

nand = test.shape[0] - test.dropna().shape[0]

print ("%d rows have missing values in the test data" %nand) 2399 rows have missing values in the train data 1221 rows have missing values in the test data.

We should now look for those columns that have any missing values.

#Only 3 columns have missing values

train.isnull().sum()

age0

workclass1836

fnlwgt0

education0

education.num0

marital.status0

occupation1843

relationship0

race0

sex0

capital.gain0

capital.loss0

hours.per.week0

native.country583

target0

dtype: int64

Using the character variables, let us now count the number of values in the data set that are unique.

```
cat = train.select_dtypes(include=['O'])

cat.apply(pd.Series.nunique)

workclass8

education16

marital.status7

occupation14

relationship6

race5

sex2

native.country41

target2

dtype: int64
```

We learned in an earlier section how to work with missing data in the data set. Let us now substitute the missing values with other values.

```
#Education

train.workclass.value_counts(sort=True)

train.workclass.fillna('Private',inplace=True)

#Occupation
```

```
train.occupation.value_counts(sort=True)

train.occupation.fillna('Prof-specialty',inplace=True)

#Native Country

train['native.country'].value_counts(sort=True)

train['native.country'].fillna('United-States',inplace=True)
```

We will now need to check if there are any values missing in the data set.

```
train.isnull().sum()

age0

workclass0

fnlwgt0

education0

education.num0

marital.status0

occupation0

relationship0

race0

sex0

capital.gain0

capital.loss0

hours.per.week0

native.country0
```

target0

dtype: int64

We will now look at the target variable to check if there is any issue within the data set.

#Check proportion of target variable

train.target.value_counts()/train.shape[0]

<=50K 0.75919

>50K 0.24081

Name: target, dtype: float64

We can see that seventy-five percent of the variables in this data set belong to the <=50k class. This means that the model will give you a result with seventy-five percent accuracy, even if it is providing you with a rough estimate. This is amazing, isn't it? Let us now create a crosstab where we will check education using the target variable. This will help us identify if the target variable is affected by education.

pd.crosstab(train.education,
train.target,margins=True)/train.shape[0]

target<=50K>50KAll

education

10th0.0267500.0019040.028654

11th0.0342430.0018430.036086

12th0.0122850.0010130.013298

1st-4th0.0049750.0001840.005160

5th-6th0.0097360.0004910.010227

7th-8th0.0186110.0012280.019840

9th0.0149570.0008290.015786

Assoc-acdm0.0246310.0081390.032769

Assoc-voc0.0313570.0110870.042443

Bachelors0.0962500.0682100.164461

Doctorate0.0032860.0093980.012684

HS-grad0.2710600.0514420.322502

Masters0.0234640.0294520.052916

Preschool0.0015660.0000000.001566

Prof-school0.0046990.0129910.017690

Some-college0.1813210.0425970.223918

All0.7591900.2408101.000000

From the above data, we can see that out of seventy-five percent of the people with a salary above 50k, at least twenty-seven percent were high school graduates. This is accurate since people with a lower level of education are not expected to earn more. On the other hand, out of the twenty-five percent of the people with a salary of 50k, five percent of them are high-school graduates while six percent have a bachelor's degree. We need to be concerned with this pattern, and we should therefore, look at all the variables before we make a conclusion.

You have come quite far in this book, and are probably wondering how you can build a machine learning model in Python. The next few chapters focus on building machine learning models using different algorithms. Let us look at a small part of building a machine learning model in this chapter. We will be using the Scikit-learn library since this library makes it easier to work with numerical data. Therefore, the primary objective is to convert all the variables in the data set into numeric data using the function 'labelencoder.' This function will help you assign a variable to any number. For instance, if the variable color is present in the data set, and there are only three colors in that set, namely red, blue, and green, we can assign the function to label red as zero, blue as one, and green as two.

```
#Load sklearn and encode all object type variables

from sklearn import preprocessing

for x in train.columns:

if train[x].dtype == 'object':

lbl = preprocessing.LabelEncoder()

lbl.fit(list(train[x].values))

train[x] = lbl.transform(list(train[x].values))
```

We will now look at the different changes that have been applied to the data set.

```
train.head()
```

ageworkclassfnlwgteducationeducation.nummarital.statusoccup
ationrelationshipracesexcapital.gaincapit
al.losshours.per.weeknative.countrytarget

03967751691340141217404038 0

15058331191323041001338 0

23832156461190514100403 8 0

35332347211725021004038 0

42833384099132952000404 0

If you pay close attention to the output, you will notice that every variable has been converted into the numeric data type.

```
#<50K = 0 and >50K = 1
train.target.value_counts()
24720
1 7841
```

Name: target, dtype: int64 Building a Random Forest Model

We are now going to test the accuracy of the model using a random forest model.

```
from sklearn.model_selection import train_test_split
from sklearn.ensemble import RandomForestClassifier
from sklearn.cross_validation import cross_val_score
from sklearn.metrics import accuracy_score
y = train['target'] del train['target'] X = train
```

```
X_train,X_test,y_train,y_test =
train_test_split(X,y,test_size=0.3,random_state=1,stratify=y)
#Train the RF classifier

clf = RandomForestClassifier(n_estimators = 500, max_depth =
6) clf.fit(X_train,y_train)

RandomForestClassifier(bootstrap=True, class_weight=None,
criterion='gini', max_depth=6, max_features='auto',
max_leaf_nodes=None, min_impurity_split=1e-07,
min_samples_leaf=1, min_samples_split=2,
min_weight_fraction_leaf=0.0, n_estimators=500, n_jobs=1,
oob_score=False, random_state=None, verbose=0,
warm_start=False)

clf.predict(X_test)
```

We will now check the accuracy of the model on the basis of some predictions that are want to make about the data set.

```
#Make prediction and check model's accuracy

prediction = clf.predict(X_test)

acc = accuracy_score(np.array(y_test),prediction)

print ('The accuracy of Random Forest is {}'.format(acc))

The accuracy of Random Forest is 0.85198075545.
```

The above algorithm will give us an accuracy of 85%. If you want to improve the accuracy, you will need to make some tweaks to the program. The training data set is divided into two parts, and the predictions are made using the second part of the data set. For the sake of practice, you should use this model and try to predict the outcome for the data that we had initially loaded into Python. Ensure that you follow all the steps that have been given in this chapter to complete the exercise.

# Chapter 9

# Building A Machine Learning Model Using Scikit-Learn

In this chapter, we will look at how we can build a machine learning model using Scikit-learn in Python. To do this, you will first need to load the SciPy and NumPy directories which will ensure that the Scikit-learn library works well in Python. You should ensure that you load these directories before you install the Scikit-learn library in your system. You can install Scikit-learn in your system using the following pip:

pip install -U Scikit-learn

Let us now start building the machine learning model.

## Step One: Load The Data Set

You will find the following components in every data set:

### *Features*

A feature is also called an attribute, predictor, or input, and it is the data point or variable that is present in the data set. You can have more than one feature in a data set, and these features are represented in the form of a matrix in the model. Every feature is assigned a name, and the list of names can be found using feature names.

### Response

A response is also known as an output, target, or label. The model will calculate the value of this variable using the feature or input variable. You will only have a single output or response variable, and this variable is represented using the response vector. The variable target names list will contain the list of values that can be given to the output or response variable.

### Loading The Example Data Sets

Numerous example data sets can be found in the Scikit-learn library, namely the Boston House Price data set which is used to build regression models and the digits and iris data sets to build classification models. If you do not have these in your system, you can download them using the following links:

- Boston House Prices:
  http://archive.ics.uci.edu/ml/datasets/Housing

- Iris: https://en.wikipedia.org/wiki/Iris_flower_data_set

- Digits: http://archive.ics.uci.edu/ml/datasets/Pen-Based+Recognition+of+Handwritten+Digits

If you want to extract the data sets through Scikit-learn, you can use the following code:

```
#Load the iris data set as an example from sklearn.datasets import load_iris iris = load_iris()
```

```
#Store the feature matrix (X) and response vector (y) X = iris.data
```

```
y = iris.target
```

```
#Store the feature and target names
```

```
feature_names = iris.feature_names
```

```
target_names = iris.target_names
```

```
#Printing features and target names of our data set
```

```
print("Feature names:", feature_names)
```

```
print("Target names:", target_names)
```

```
X and y are numpy arrays print("\nType of X is:", type(X))
```

```
printing first 5 input rows print("\nFirst 5 rows of X:\n", X[:5])
```
The output for the above code is:

Feature names: ['sepal length (cm)','sepal width (cm)', 'petal length (cm)','petal width (cm)']

Target names: ['setosa' 'versicolor' 'virginica'] Type of X is:

First 5 rows of X: [[ 5.1 3.5 1.4 0.2] [ 4.9 3. 1.4 0.2] [ 4.7 3.2 1.3 0.2] [ 4.6 3.1 1.5 0.2] [ 5. 3.6 1.4 0.2]]

## Loading An External Data Set

Let us now look at how you can load an external data set into the Scikit-learn library. For this, we will need to use the Pandas library since this allows us to manipulate the data easily. These manipulations have been described in the previous chapter. To load an external data set, you can use the following command:

pip install pandas

The data set used in the example below is downloaded from the following location:

http://www.sharecsv.com/dl/327fb8f66f90a98c2ed4454665efae
9d/weather.csv

import pandas as pd

#Reading csv file

data = pd.read_csv('weather.csv')

shape of data set print("Shape:", data.shape)

column names print("\nFeatures:", data.columns)

storing the feature matrix (X) and response vector (y) X =
data[data.columns[:-1]]

y = data[data.columns[-1]]

printing first 5 rows of feature matrix

print("\nFeature matrix:\n", X.head())

'printing first 5 values of response vector

print("\nResponse vector:\n", y.head()) The output for the above code is:

Shape: (14, 5)

Features: Index([u'Outlook', u'Temperature', u'Humidity', u'Windy', u'Play'], dtype='object')

Feature matrix:

Outlook Temperature Humidity Windy 0 overcast hot high False

1 overcast cool normal True

2 overcast mild high True

3 overcast hot normal False

4 rainy mild high False Response vector:

0 yes

1 yes

2 yes

3 yes

4 yes

Name: Play, dtype: object

## Step Two: Splitting The Data Set

It is necessary that we determine the accuracy of the model. For this, you should first train the model using the training data set and test the accuracy of the model using the same data set. The prediction results or the outcomes are used to test the accuracy and performance of the model. There are numerous disadvantages to testing the accuracy of the model in this manner:

- You cannot maximize or improve the performance and accuracy of the model if you use the same data set to train and test the accuracy of the model.

- When you use the training data set to test the accuracy of the model, you tend to develop an overly complex model that cannot be used on any other data set.

- If you build a complex model, it will tend to overfit the data.

It is for this reason that the data set should be divided into two sections or parts. We will then use one part to train (training data set) the model and the other part to test (testing data set) the model. You can evaluate the performance of the model with the help of the test data set.

There are two advantages to using this method:

- The model can be trained and tested using different data sets. This will help us assess the accuracy of the model.

- The accuracy of the predictions can be tested since we are only provided the response value to the model for the test data set.

Let us look at the following example:

```
#Load the iris data set as an example
from sklearn.datasets import load_iris
iris = load_iris()
store the feature matrix (X) and response vector (y) X = iris.data
y = iris.target
```

'The data set is being split into the variables X and Y (training data set and testing data set) using the sklearn.model_selection

```
import train_test_split
X_train, X_test, y_train, y_test = train_test_split(X, y,
    test_size=0.4, random_state=1)
printing the shapes of the new X objects
print(X_train.shape)
print(X_test.shape)
printing the shapes of the new y objects print(y_train.shape)
    print(y_test.shape)
The output for the code above is: (90L, 4L)
(60L, 4L) (90L,) (60L,)
```

The arguments that are taken by the function train_test_split will take different arguments, which have been explained below:

- Test Size: This variable will provide the information on the ratio of the test data that we are selecting from the full data

147

set. For instance, if the data set has 150 rows and the size that we have selected is 0.4, the value of X will be 60 rows (150*0.4).

- Random_State: The data set that you have split will not change if you use a random number for this parameter. You should remember this function and use it when you need to obtain the same results. This will allow you to test the performance of the model.

- Variables X and Y: The variables X and Y represent the features and the responses. We will need to work on splitting these variables.

## Step Three: Training The Model

We will now need to train the machine learning model with the training data set. There are numerous machine learning algorithms that you can use through Scikit-learn. Since these algorithms are a part of separate packages, they have a consistent method that is used to predict the accuracy, fit the data, etc. The example below uses the K Nearest Neighbors Classifier package.

load the iris data set as an example from sklearn.datasets import load_iris iris = load_iris()

store the feature matrix (X) and response vector (y) X = iris.data

y = iris.target

splitting X and y into training and testing sets from sklearn.model_selection import train_test_split

```
X_train, X_test, y_train, y_test = train_test_split(X, y,
test_size=0.4, random_state=1)
```

#Training the model on training set

```
from sklearn.neighbors import KNeighborsClassifier

knn = KNeighborsClassifier(n_neighbors=3)

knn.fit(X_train, y_train)
```

making predictions on the testing set y_pred = knn.predict(X_test)

comparing actual response values (y_test) with predicted response values (y_pred) from sklearn import metrics

```
print("kNN model accuracy:", metrics.accuracy_score(y_test, y_pred))
```

making prediction for out of sample data

```
sample = [[3, 5, 4, 2], [2, 3, 5, 4]]

preds = knn.predict(sample)

pred_species = [iris.target_names[p] for p in preds]
print("Predictions:", pred_species)
```

#Saving the model

```
from sklearn.externals import joblib

joblib.dump(knn, 'iris_knn.pkl')
```

The output of the code above will be:

kNN model accuracy: 0.983333333333

Predictions: ['versicolor', 'virginica']

# Chapter 10

# Supervised Algorithms Implementation

In the introduction to machine learning, we learned that there are different applications of machine learning. Depending on the application that you want to build, there are different categories of learning like supervised learning, unsupervised learning, and reinforced learning.

If you recollect, there are different algorithms that have the sign under each of these categories. In this chapter we will look at some of the algorithms that are used under the supervised machine learning category. We will first look at the regression algorithm, and look at two types of regression, namely linear regression and multiple regression. We will see how we can build these algorithms in Python.

The simplest machine learning algorithms used in supervised learning algorithm can be classified into two classes:

- Regression Algorithms

- Classification Algorithms

Before we delve into learning how to build a model in Python, let us look at a simple linear regression model example to understand these concepts clearly. The basic idea of any machine learning algorithm is to enable the machine to predict a sample output using some training data set which also provides information on the necessary outputs. The machine should learn to identify the relationship between the input and output variables using the training data set. It will then need to protect the outcome for any new data sets or inputs given.

The example below is simple to understand; we will ask the machine to suggest whether a person should carry an umbrella or not depending on the weather. The following table consists of the sample training data set.

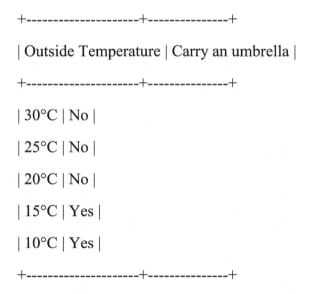

```
+--------------------+--------------+

| Outside Temperature | Carry an umbrella |

+--------------------+--------------+

| 30°C | No |
| 25°C | No |
| 20°C | No |
| 15°C | Yes |
| 10°C | Yes |

+--------------------+--------------+
```

Our mind is trained to look at the temperature and determine what the output should be. This means that we will look at the weather outside and determine whether or not we need to carry an umbrella. Let us now try to model this decision by using an algebraic equation. You can use this equation to train the machine to make such a decision.

For this, we will need to use this Scikit-learn library which is one of the most trusted Python libraries for machine learning models. Consider the following sample set:

| x1 | x2 | x3 | y |
|----|----|----|-----|
| 1  | 2  | 3  | 14  |
| 4  | 5  | 6  | 32  |
| 11 | 12 | 13 | 74  |
| 21 | 22 | 23 | 134 |
| 5  | 5  | 5  | 30  |

If you look at the above table, you can insert the mathematical model or the equation to obtain the output which should be:  $y = (x1 + 2*x2 + 3*x3)$.

To generate the training data set:

```
from random import randint
TRAIN_SET_LIMIT = 1000
TRAIN_SET_COUNT = 100
TRAIN_INPUT = list()
TRAIN_OUTPUT = list()
```

```
for i in range(TRAIN_SET_COUNT):

a = randint(0, TRAIN_SET_LIMIT)

b = randint(0, TRAIN_SET_LIMIT)

c = randint(0, TRAIN_SET_LIMIT)

op = a + (2*b) + (3*c)

TRAIN_INPUT.append([a, b, c])

TRAIN_OUTPUT.append(op)
```

Train the model:

```
from sklearn.linear_model import LinearRegression

predictor = LinearRegression(n_jobs=-1)

predictor.fit(X=TRAIN_INPUT, y=TRAIN_OUTPUT)
```

once a system is very, you should fast sample test data set in the following format, [ [10, 20, 30]], and observe the output. This must be 10+20*2+30*2 and output must be 140

```
X_TEST = [[10, 20, 30]]

outcome = predictor.predict(X=X_TEST)

coefficients = predictor.coef_

print('Outcome : {}\nCoefficients : {}'.format(outcome,
coefficients))
```

Output

Outcome = [140]

Coefficients = [1.2.3]

We have now successfully implemented the model, trained, and observed the prediction of the output for any new input based on a mathematical linear equation.

## Regression Algorithm

Regression is a supervised learning algorithm. In this model, we will first give inputs to the machine and we will decide an output which is a numeric value. The interest is not to learn what the class of the variable will be, but to understand the numeric function that will describe the data. The objective is to then use this equation to generate any estimates.

The most common and simplest regression model is the linear regression model. This is a model that most engineers prefer to use to derive a predictive function. This model should be used when there is a correlation coefficient that you can use to predict the results.

This function is used to create a scatter plot of the data points using the input that is given. The scatter plot will also include a straight line. This method will help the engineer and the machine identify whether there is a linear relation between two or more variables.

The following mathematical formula is used to calculate the slope of a straight line: $Y = mx + c$.

This is a popular algebraic equation which can be used to identify or explain the linear relationship between variables. This equation can also be used to explain the concept of linear regression to a machine. In the above equation, we have a dependent variable, the function of a variable, and another variable which is the independent variable.

The objective of this method is to identify a function which will help you determine how two variables are related. In every data set, you are given a list of values in the row and column format. You can plot this data on the x and y axes of a graph.

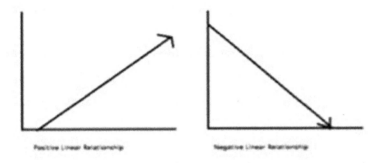

Positive Linear Relationship          Negative Linear Relationship

*Image: Illustration to depict positive and negative linear regression.*

Linear regression is used to observe how the dependent variable increases or decreases when the independent variable increases or decreases.

In the image above, you can see that a linear relationship can either be negative or positive. A positive slope indicates that the value of the dependent variable will go up or down when the value of the independent variable goes up or down.

A negative slope indicates that the value of the dependent variable will go up when the value of the independent variable goes down, and vice versa. Let us now go back to the algebraic equation to calculate the slope of a line, and understand how you can implement this in a regression model in Python.

We saw that the variables X and Y will have a relationship, but this does not necessarily have to be true. In a simple linear regression model, the model we build is based on the data and we do not need to identify the relationship between the variables X and Y. We also do not require that the relationship between the variables be exactly linear, since we will include residuals which represent the errors.

The aim is to use continuous data, identify an equation that best fits the data, and extrapolate or forecast a specific value for the future. In the case of simple linear regression models, we will do this by creating a line of best fit.

One of the popular applications of a linear regression model is to predict the stock prices on real estate market prices. Regression is a type of supervised learning; the engineer must train the machine by providing a training data set which talks about the features and the corresponding output for those features. The engineer must feed the machine with numerous search data sets. This will help the machine predict the output if any new input is given.

There are many data sets available on the Internet, and you can pick the example of a stock market data set for the sample code below. For this data set, you need to install and import the quandl package.

Open your Python window and copy the following script and execute it from the terminal. This will help you pull the stock data set from the Internet.

```
import pandas as pd
import Quandl
df = Quandl.get("WIKI/GOOGL")
print(df.head())
```

Please note to check the case of the library "quandl" or "Quandl" depending on the version of Python you are using.

```
Open High Low Close Volume Ex-Dividend \
Date
2004-08-19 100.00 104.06 95.96 100.34 44659000 0
2004-08-20 101.01 109.08 100.50 108.31 22834300 0
2004-08-23 110.75 113.48 109.05 109.40 18256100 0
2004-08-24 111.24 111.60 103.57 104.87 15247300 0
2004-08-25 104.96 108.00 103.88 106.00 9188600 0

 Split Ratio Adj. Open Adj. High Adj. Low Adj. Close \
Date
2004-08-19 1 50.000 52.03 47.980 50.170
2004-08-20 1 50.505 54.54 50.250 54.155
2004-08-23 1 55.375 56.74 54.525 54.700
2004-08-24 1 55.620 55.80 51.785 52.435
```

2004-08-25 1 52.480 54.00 51.940 53.000

Adj. Volume

Date

2004-08-19 44659000

2004-08-20 22834300

2004-08-23 18256100

2004-08-24 15247300

2004-08-25 9188600

Is the sample data pulled from the Internet?

Remember the lesson from the previous chapter? Yes, the first step is to scrub, clean, and prepare the data set. One will notice that there are some redundancies and discrepancies in the pulled data set. The same can be rectified by adding the following line of code to the Python script:

```
df = df[['Adj. Open', 'Adj. High', 'Adj. Low', 'Adj. Close', 'Adj. Volume']]
```

And if we were to apply a bit of common sense, one can understand that not all of this data is useful and the cleaned data set can further be transformed for better results using the piece of code given below:

```
df['HL_PCT'] = (df['Adj. High'] - df['Adj. Low']) / df['Adj. Close'] * 100.0
```

158

And the following piece of code defines dataframes and interprets the data output:

```
df['PCT_change'] = (df['Adj. Close'] - df['Adj. Open']) / df['Adj. Open'] * 100.0

df = df[['Adj. Close', 'HL_PCT', 'PCT_change', 'Adj. Volume']]

print(df.head())
```

The output will look like this:

```
Adj. Close HL_PCT PCT_change Adj. Volume
Date
2004-08-19 50.170 8.072553 0.340000 44659000
2004-08-20 54.155 7.921706 7.227007 22834300
2004-08-23 54.700 4.049360 -1.218962 18256100
2004-08-24 52.435 7.657099 -5.726357 15247300
2004-08-25 53.000 3.886792 0.990854 9188600
```

With this, we have our data set ready, which we will now have to convert to array format that will be understandable by the Scikit library, which we will be using to perform actual regression functions.

For us to proceed further, add the following lines of code to the Python script file. These lines essentially import libraries which will be required for further functionalities.

```
import Quandl, math
```

```
import numpy as np

import pandas as pd

from sklearn import preprocessing, cross_validation, svm

from sklearn.linear_model import LinearRegression
```

At this point, the Python script file must look something like this:

```
import Quandl, math

import numpy as np

import pandas as pd

from sklearn import preprocessing, cross_validation, svm

from sklearn.linear_model import LinearRegression

df = Quandl.get("WIKI/GOOGL")

df = df[['Adj. Open', 'Adj. High', 'Adj. Low', 'Adj. Close', 'Adj. Volume']]

df['HL_PCT'] = (df['Adj. High'] - df['Adj. Low']) / df['Adj. Close'] * 100.0

df['PCT_change'] = (df['Adj. Close'] - df['Adj. Open']) / df['Adj. Open'] * 100.0

df = df[['Adj. Close', 'HL_PCT', 'PCT_change', 'Adj. Volume']]

print(df.head())
```

Now, if we recollect, we are at the stage ready to cross validate our cleaned and prepared data, for which we need to add the following lines, which will feed the data as a feature and label tuple to the classifier machine learning model. The feature can be defined as 'descriptive attributes,' while labels are the values that we are looking to predict with our machine learning models.

```
forecast_col = 'Adj. Close'

df.fillna(value=-99999, inplace=True)

forecast_out = int(math.ceil(0.01 * len(df)))

df['label'] = df[forecast_col].shift(-forecast_out)
```

With the above few lines of code, we've defined what we want to forecast. The next steps are to train and test our model.

At this point, we can use the dropna function and then proceed to convert the data to numpy array format, which is the expected data format by Scikit library functions that we will be subsequently using.

```
df.dropna(inplace=True)

X = np.array(df.drop(['label'], 1))

Y = np.array(df['label'])

X = preprocessing.scale(X)

Y = np.array(df['label'])
```

We have now created the label, array, and preprocessed the data set. We will now use the svm model and classifier model clf available in the Scikit toolkit to predict and print how robust the model is - the accuracy and reliability of it using the confidence functions.

```
X_train, X_test, y_train, y_test =
cross_validation.train_test_split(X, y, test_size=0.2)

clf = svm.SVR()

clf.fit(X_train, y_train)

confidence = clf.score(X_test, y_test)

print(confidence)
```

One can rerun the same script using the linear regression classifier instead of svm as follows:

```
clf = LinearRegression()
```

The next steps are to forecast and predict, for which the following lines of code need to be added to existing script:

```
forecast_set = clf.predict(X_lately)

print(forecast_set, confidence, forecast_out)
```

The output:

```
[ 745.67829395  737.55633261  736.32921413  717.03929303
718.59047951

 731.26376715  737.84381394  751.28161162  756.31775293
756.76751056

 763.20185946  764.52651181  760.91320031  768.0072636
766.67038016

 763.83749414  761.36173409  760.08514166  770.61581391
774.13939706
```

768.78733341  775.04458624  771.10782342  765.13955723
773.93369548

766.05507556  765.4984563  763.59630529  770.0057166
777.60915879] 0.956987938167 30

The next step is to import and Matplotlib to plot the scatter plot, which is beyond the scope of this book.

Thus linear regression is used in varied applications and domains ranging from economics to biology to predict trend lines of oil prices, GDP, house prices, how much a country should spend on imports, etc.

Correlation formulas can be used to predict how close to reality the prediction obtained from linear regression models is.

Let us look at another very simple linear regression model example to understand this very clearly.

To reiterate the basic idea of any machine learning algorithm is that the system is exposed to a very large number of training data sets and also shows a large sample of expected outputs. Based on these training data sets, the machine learns to figure out the relationship between the input and output and based on this also learns to predict for new inputs given.

Below is a very primitive example of when the system suggests whether the user needs an umbrella or not depending on the weather of the day. Let us say, the following table contains a sample set of training data.

```
+----------------------+----------------+
| Outside Temperature  | Grab an umbrella |
+----------------------+----------------+
| 30°C | No  |
| 25°C | No  |
| 20°C | No  |
| 15°C | Yes |
| 10°C | Yes |
+----------------------+----------------+
```

As an average human being, our mind is trained to look at the input temperature and determine the output - the decision to grab an umbrella or not. So assume the temperature is 10°C, you might want to carry an umbrella expecting a snowstorm or rainstorm. Let us now try to model this decision-making process into an algebraic equation so that a machine can also be trained to take such a decision when given this data set.

For this, we will need to use the trusted Python Library for machine learning implementations: Scikit-learn. And consider the following sample data set.

| x1 | x2 | x3 | y |
|----|----|----|----|
| 1  | 2  | 3  | 14 |
| 4  | 5  | 6  | 32 |
| 11 | 12 | 13 | 74 |

| 21 | 22 | 23 | 134 |
| 5 | 5 | 5 | 30 |

Looking at the table one can infer the mathematical model or algebraic equation to get the output y = (x1 + 2*x2 + 3*x3).

To generate the training data set

```
from random import randint
TRAIN_SET_LIMIT = 1000
TRAIN_SET_COUNT = 100
TRAIN_INPUT = list()
TRAIN_OUTPUT = list()
for i in range(TRAIN_SET_COUNT):
a = randint(0, TRAIN_SET_LIMIT)
b = randint(0, TRAIN_SET_LIMIT)
c = randint(0, TRAIN_SET_LIMIT)
op = a + (2*b) + (3*c)
TRAIN_INPUT.append([a, b, c])
TRAIN_OUTPUT.append(op)
```

Train the model:

```
from sklearn.linear_model import LinearRegression
predictor = LinearRegression(n_jobs=-1)
predictor.fit(X=TRAIN_INPUT, y=TRAIN_OUTPUT)
```

Once the system is ready, pass a sample test data in the following format of a tuple [ [10, 20, 30]] and observe the output. According to our algebraic equation, this must be 10+20*2+30*2 and the output must be 140.

X_TEST = [[10, 20, 30]]

outcome = predictor.predict(X=X_TEST)

coefficients = predictor.coef_

print('Outcome: {}\nCoefficients: {}'.format(outcome, coefficients))

Output

Outcome = [140]

Coefficients = [1.2.3]

We have now developed a linear regression model, trained it, and predicted the output for a new data set using the basic linear equation.

## Multiple Regression

The previous section covered linear regression modeling, where we looked at one predictor variable and one response variable. The only interest that data miners have is on the relationship that exists between a set of predictor variables and a target variable. Most applications built for data mining have a lot of data, with some sets including thousands or millions of variables, of which most have a linear relationship with the response or target variable. That is when a data miner would prefer to use a multiple linear regression model.

These models provide improved accuracy and precision on prediction and estimation, similar to the improved accuracy of regression estimates over bivariate or univariate estimates.

Multiple regression models often use linear surfaces like planes and hyperplanes to determine the relationship between the variables in the data set. These planes are used to identify the relationship that exists between the predictor variable and the target variable. The predictor variables or the input variables can be discrete or continuous. If the data set is categorical, the variables will be used as indicator variables alone. In a simple linear regression model, a straight line of dimension is used to estimate the relationship between the predictor and response variable. If one wants to evaluate the relationship between an input or predictor variable and the output or response variable visually, you should plot the data on a plane.

Data miners should always ensure that they prevent multicollinearity in the data. Multicollinearity is a condition where some or all of the independent variables or predictor variables are correlated. If this is the case, it will lead to some differences in the solution space. This will mean that you will not receive a coherent result. Therefore, it is important that you check the data for collinearity with a t-test, and an f-test to check the effect of collinearity on the output.

The high variability associated with the estimates for different regression coefficients means that different samples may produce coefficient estimates with widely different values. For example, some samples may produce a positive coefficient for the variable x1, while the other samples may produce a negative coefficient estimate. This is a situation that is unacceptable since you must identify and explain the relationship between the variables individually. If there is a chance to avoid such instability when highly correlated variables are included, those variables will emphasize a particular component of the model being used because these elements are being counted twice. If you want to ignore multicollinearity, you should always look at the structure of correlation between the predictor variables. You should ignore the target variables for the moment.

We should always look for some correlation between the predictor variables. If you do not want to look at the correlation between the input variables, you should look for a way to identify the collinearity in the data set. This can be done by using the variance inflation factors that you obtain through the results. You must identify a way to standardize the variables in the data set to ensure that a change in one variable does not affect every other variable, thereby affecting the performance of the model.

From pandas import DataFrame ("Example of Multiple," 2019)

From sklearn import linear_model

import tkinter as tk

import matplotlib.pyplot as plt

From matplotlib.backends.backend_tkagg import FigureCanvasTkAgg

```python
Stock_Market = {'Year':
[2017,2017,2017,2017,2017,2017,2017,2017,2017,2017,2017,2
017,2016,2016,2016,2016,2016,2016,2016,2016,2016,2016,201
6,2016],

        'Month':
[12,11,10,9,8,7,6,5,4,3,2,1,12,11,10,9,8,7,6,5,4,3,2,1],

        'Interest_Rate':
[2.75,2.5,2.5,2.5,2.5,2.5,2.5,2.25,2.25,2.25,2,2,2,1.75,1.75,1.75,
1.75,1.75,1.75,1.75,1.75,1.75,1.75,1.75],

        'Unemployment_Rate':
[5.3,5.3,5.3,5.3,5.4,5.6,5.5,5.5,5.5,5.6,5.7,5.9,6,5.9,5.8,6.1,6.2,6
.1,6.1,6.1,5.9,6.2,6.2,6.1],

        'Stock_Index_Price':
[1464,1394,1357,1293,1256,1254,1234,1195,1159,1167,1130,1
075,1047,965,943,958,971,949,884,866,876,822,704,719]

        }


df =
DataFrame(Stock_Market,columns=['Year','Month','Interest_Ra
te','Unemployment_Rate','Stock_Index_Price'])


#Here we have two input variables for multiple regression. If
you just want to use one variable for simple linear regression,
then use X = df['Interest_Rate'] for example. Alternatively, you
may add additional variables within the brackets.
```

```
X = df[['Interest_Rate','Unemployment_Rate']].astype(float)


#Output variable (what we are trying to predict)

Y = df['Stock_Index_Price'].astype(float)

#With sklearn

regr = linear_model.LinearRegression()

regr.fit(X, Y)


print('Intercept: \n', regr.intercept_)

print('Coefficients: \n', regr.coef_)



 #Tkinter GUI

root= tk.Tk()


canvas1 = tk.Canvas(root, width = 500, height = 300)

canvas1.pack()


#With sklearn

Intercept_result = ('Intercept: ', regr.intercept_)

label_Intercept = tk.Label(root, text=Intercept_result, justify =
'center')
```

```python
canvas1.create_window(260, 220, window=label_Intercept)


#With sklearn
Coefficients_result = ('Coefficients: ', regr.coef_)
label_Coefficients = tk.Label(root, text=Coefficients_result,
justify = 'center')
canvas1.create_window(260, 240, window=label_Coefficients)



#New_Interest_Rate label and input box
label1 = tk.Label(root, text='Type Interest Rate: ')
canvas1.create_window(100, 100, window=label1)


entry1 = tk.Entry (root) #Create 1st entry box
canvas1.create_window(270, 100, window=entry1)


#New_Unemployment_Rate label and input box
label2 = tk.Label(root, text=' Type Unemployment Rate: ')
canvas1.create_window(120, 120, window=label2)


entry2 = tk.Entry (root) #Create 2nd entry box
canvas1.create_window(270, 120, window=entry2)
```

```python
def values():
    global New_Interest_Rate #Our 1st input variable
    New_Interest_Rate = float(entry1.get())


    global New_Unemployment_Rate #Our 2nd input variable
    New_Unemployment_Rate = float(entry2.get())


    Prediction_result  = ('Predicted Stock Index Price: ',
regr.predict([[New_Interest_Rate
,New_Unemployment_Rate]]))
    label_Prediction = tk.Label(root, text= Prediction_result,
bg='orange')
    canvas1.create_window(260, 280, window=label_Prediction)


button1 = tk.Button (root, text='Predict Stock Index
Price',command=values, bg='orange') #Button to call the
'values' command above
canvas1.create_window(270, 150, window=button1)


#Plot 1st scatter
figure3 = plt.Figure(figsize=(5,4), dpi=100)
ax3 = figure3.add_subplot(111)
```

```
ax3.scatter(df['Interest_Rate'].astype(float),df['Stock_Index_Pri
ce'].astype(float), color = 'r')

scatter3 = FigureCanvasTkAgg(figure3, root)

scatter3.get_tk_widget().pack(side=tk.RIGHT, fill=tk.BOTH)

ax3.legend()

ax3.set_xlabel('Interest Rate')

ax3.set_title('Interest Rate Vs. Stock Index Price')


#Plot 2nd scatter

figure4 = plt.Figure(figsize=(5,4), dpi=100)

ax4 = figure4.add_subplot(111)

ax4.scatter(df['Unemployment_Rate'].astype(float),df['Stock_In
dex_Price'].astype(float), color = 'g')

scatter4 = FigureCanvasTkAgg(figure4, root)

scatter4.get_tk_widget().pack(side=tk.RIGHT, fill=tk.BOTH)

ax4.legend()

ax4.set_xlabel('Unemployment_Rate')

ax4.set_title('Unemployment_Rate Vs. Stock Index Price')


root.mainloop()
```

You can add the code in the above section to a .py file and execute that script through a terminal. Alternatively, you can download the data set into a working directory and run the script so you can obtain the output. The output will also include a scatter plot.

## Classification Algorithm - Decision Trees

Decision trees are a classic example of a classification algorithm. This method was used in the past to identify the probability of outcomes. A decision tree algorithm works on both continuous and categorical data, and is an example of a supervised machine learning algorithm. This algorithm is often used to predict the class of different input data. The k-nearest algorithm is another popular classification algorithm used in machine learning. In this algorithm, the objective is to predict the category of any target variable using the variables similar to the input variable as a classification attribute.

The decision tree algorithm works on the basis of a decision rule that is mentioned to the model by the engineer while training the model. If you are familiar with programming languages, you will realize that this algorithm has the same characteristics as the conditional statements. The format of a decision tree is different when compared to the conditional statements in a programming language. The decision tree, as the name suggests, is a branch based chart, and is a simple algorithm that any person can understand and use. Let us assume that you want to identify a way to define whether an email is spam or important. To do this, you must give the model some predefined rules that it should follow.

The machine can use any branch in the decision tree to obtain the output to a specific problem. The information presented in the tree is sufficient to provide the result for a specific problem. The branches in the tree will depict the action that the machine will take.

Some key advantages of using decision trees are:

### *Simple to understand and interpret and easy to visualize*

When you use this model you will require minimal or no data preparation. However, when it comes to other algorithms you will need to prepare the data set to ensure that the variables are normalized. You may also need to create or insert dummy values where there are missing items in the data set. This reduces the time and the cost that goes into developing this machine learning model. It is, however, important to know that this model will need missing data to be filled up, otherwise you will generate an error. It will then stop computing the data set.

The number of data points determines the cost of execution. The relationship of cost to number of data is logarithmic to train the data model. Another advantage of using this model is that it will work well with both categorical and numerical data. Many other algorithms can work with only one format.

### *Ability to handle multi-output problems*

Decision trees use the white box mode. This means that the tree will always tell you how it arrived at a solution using Boolean logic equations. In the case of algorithms that are based on the black box model, it is difficult to understand how the output was derived.

Another advantage of a decision tree is that it will always evaluate a model using numerous statistical trails. This makes the model more reliable when compared to others.

This model will also perform well when the assumptions are slightly violated if you apply them to the actual data set or model. This will ensure that the algorithm is flexible and provides results regardless of the variance.

Some disadvantages of using a decision tree includes:

1. A decision tree can create overly complex trees that do not generalize data well - basically it is the problem of overfitting. This can be avoided using techniques like pruning (literally like pruning the branch of a tree, but this is currently not supported in Python libraries) - the task involves setting up a few samples needed at a leaf node or setting the highest depth a tree can grow to, thus limiting the problem of overfitting.

2. The trees become unstable because of small variations in the input data, resulting in an entirely different tree generating. This issue can be avoided by using a decision tree within an ensemble.

3. NP-Complete problem - a very common theoretical computer science problem can be a hindrance in the attempt to design the most optimal decision tree, because under several aspects, the optimality can become affected. As a

result, heuristic algorithms, such as greedy algorithms, where local optimal decisions at each node become an issue. Teaching multiple trees to a collaborative learner can again reduce the effect of this issue and the feature and samples can be randomly sampled with replacements.

4. Concepts like parity, multiplexer, and XOR are difficult to express or compute using decision trees.

5. In the case of dominant classes, biased learners are developed. This is because of the imbalance within the data set which are not looked into before setting up the decision tree.

6. You have to know that the decision tree can overfit the data, if there are a large number of features. If you are using a large data set, you must ensure that you choose the right sample to model the data. Otherwise, the decision tree will have too many dimensions.

7. Decision trees are used extensively in designing intelligent home automation systems. For example, if the current temperature of the room is too low or too high, the system will adjust using decision trees. You can also model the decisions like whether a person should carry an umbrella to work or if a person should go out to play cricket.

There are two key factors:

- Entropy - this measure must be low. The entropy measures the impurity or the randomness in a sample set.

- Information Gain - This is also known as entropy reduction. This is a measure of how the entropy has changed once the data has been split. The value of the entropy reduction should be high.

The following are the key concepts that you will need to learn when you are modeling a decision tree in Python (Sharma, n.d.).

```
#Run this program on your local python

#Interpreter, provided you have installed the required libraries


#Importing the required packages

import numpy as np

import pandas as pd

from sklearn.metrics import confusion_matrix

from sklearn.cross_validation import train_test_split

from sklearn.tree import DecisionTreeClassifier

from sklearn.metrics import accuracy_score

from sklearn.metrics import classification_report
```

```python
#Function importing data set
def importdata():
    balance_data = pd.read_csv(
'https://archive.ics.uci.edu/ml/machine-learning-'+
'databases/balance-scale/balance-scale.data',
    sep= ',', header = None)

    #Printing the dataset shape
    print ("Dataset Length: ", len(balance_data))
    print ("Dataset Shape: ", balance_data.shape)

    #Printing the data set observations
    print ("Dataset: ",balance_data.head())
    return balance_data

#Function to split the data set
def splitdataset(balance_data):

    #Separating the target variable
    X = balance_data.values[:, 1:5]
    Y = balance_data.values[:, 0]
```

```python
#Splitting the data set into train and test
X_train, X_test, y_train, y_test = train_test_split(
X, Y, test_size = 0.3, random_state = 100)


return X, Y, X_train, X_test, y_train, y_test

#Function to perform training with giniIndex.
def train_using_gini(X_train, X_test, y_train):

    #Creating the classifier object
    clf_gini = DecisionTreeClassifier(criterion = "gini",
            random_state = 100,max_depth=3,
min_samples_leaf=5)


    #Performing training
    clf_gini.fit(X_train, y_train)
    return clf_gini

#Function to perform training with entropy
def tarin_using_entropy(X_train, X_test, y_train):

    #Decision tree with entropy
```

```
clf_entropy = DecisionTreeClassifier(
        criterion = "entropy", random_state = 100,
        max_depth = 3, min_samples_leaf = 5)


#Performing training
clf_entropy.fit(X_train, y_train)
return clf_entropy



#Function to make predictions
def prediction(X_test, clf_object):

    #Prediction on test with giniIndex
    y_pred = clf_object.predict(X_test)
    print("Predicted values:")
    print(y_pred)
    return y_pred


#Function to calculate accuracy
def cal_accuracy(y_test, y_pred):

    print("Confusion Matrix : ",
```

```python
        confusion_matrix(y_test, y_pred))

    print ("Accuracy : ",
    accuracy_score(y_test,y_pred)*100)

    print("Report : ",
    classification_report(y_test, y_pred))

#Driver code
def main():

    #Building Phase
    data = importdata()
    X, Y, X_train, X_test, y_train, y_test = splitdataset(data)
    clf_gini = train_using_gini(X_train, X_test, y_train)
    clf_entropy = tarin_using_entropy(X_train, X_test, y_train)

    #Operational Phase
    print("Results Using Gini Index:")

    #Prediction using gini
    y_pred_gini = prediction(X_test, clf_gini)
```

182

```
cal_accuracy(y_test, y_pred_gini)


print("Results Using Entropy:")
#Prediction using entropy
y_pred_entropy = prediction(X_test, clf_entropy)
cal_accuracy(y_test, y_pred_entropy)



#Calling main function
if __name__ == "__main__":
    main()
```

Most engineers use the k-nearest neighbor algorithm to solve a classification problem.

If you are looking to develop a code to build a model that uses the k-nearest algorithm, you should use the code in the section below. This algorithm is used to classify the data in the data set into different categories or groups using the supervised machine learning algorithm technique (Robinson, 2018).

```
import numpy as np
import matplotlib.pyplot as plt
import pandas as pd
#Importing the data set
```

```
url = "https://archive.ics.uci.edu/ml/machine-learning-
databases/iris/iris.data"


#Assign column names to the data set

names = ['sepal-length', 'sepal-width', 'petal-length', 'petal-
width', 'Class']


#Read data set to pandas DataFrame

dataset = pd.read_csv(url, names=names)

#To view the data set

dataset.head()

#Preprocessing of data

X = dataset.iloc[:, :-1].values

y = dataset.iloc[:, 4].values

#Splitting the data set

from sklearn.model_selection import train_test_split

X_train, X_test, y_train, y_test = train_test_split(X, y,
test_size=0.20)

#Feature scaling

from sklearn.preprocessing import StandardScaler

scaler = StandardScaler()

scaler.fit(X_train)
```

```
X_train = scaler.transform(X_train)

X_test = scaler.transform(X_test)

#Training the model

from sklearn.neighbors import KNeighborsClassifier

classifier = KNeighborsClassifier(n_neighbors=5)

classifier.fit(X_train, y_train)

y_pred = classifier.predict(X_test)

#Evaluating the algorithm

from sklearn.metrics import classification_report,
confusion_matrix

print(confusion_matrix(y_test, y_pred))

print(classification_report(y_test, y_pred))
```

# Chapter 11

# Unsupervised Learning Algorithms

## Clustering

In the previous sections, we looked at how a supervised learning algorithm, such as the classification and regression algorithm, is used to develop a machine learning model. In this section we will talk about the clustering unsupervised machine learning algorithm and how it can be modeled in Python.

If you can collect the right data, an unsupervised algorithm will learn to make meaningful inferences from an unlabeled data set. This is different from supervised machine learning since there is no concept of a predictor variable or a target variable that the machine has to predict. The objective here is to inform the description of every data point in the data set using the training data set and input data set.

In supervised machine learning, you are looking for the answer to 'why' based on the input data x. In unsupervised learning, however, we are looking to find what a model will predict if x is given.

In the data science domain, you often think about how the data available can be used to make predictions of view data points. There are times where you want to categorize the available information into categories of clusters and not just make predictions. The former is an example of supervised machine learning, while the latter is an example of unsupervised machine learning.

Let us look at the following example to understand this. Let us assume that you are working in a pizza shop, and you are tasked with creating a new feature to manage the order. This feature should predict the delivery time for the customer. You have historical information on the previous deliveries, which includes information about the distance travelled to deliver the pizzas, and other parameters like the time of day or week. Using this information you can predict future delivery time. This is an example of supervised machine learning.

Let us now look at a requirement. You are employed at the same pizza joint, but you are tasked with identifying the segment of your customers to run a coupon campaign. You have access to some historical data such as the name of your customers, their age, area, and other information. You can now classify these customers into different clusters based on numerous factors. This is an example of unsupervised machine learning where you are not making a prediction by simply categorizing your customers into numerous groups.

### Real Life Applications of Clustering

Many industries use large and complex data sets to perform analyses, and they use the clustering algorithm to simplify these analyses. A classic example of this would be genomics. In genomics, a cluster of genes is created by the model. This cluster is based on the properties of every gene. This type of algorithm is also used in astronomy to classify different celestial objects based on their size, distance, color, material, etc. Clustering can also be used to predict the areas prone to earthquakes. Some businesses also use the clustering algorithm for the following:

- Image segmentation
- Medical image detection
- Social media analysis
- In driving targeted advertisements
- In Netflix recommendations
- Recommendation engines
- Market segmentation
- Anomaly detection
- Search result grouping

### Classification of Clustering Algorithms

Most engineers and data scientists use clustering algorithms to solve a variety of problems. Clustering algorithms are classified into two categories depending on the classification of the input data.

## Hard Clustering

In a hard clustering algorithm, the input master key will always belong to one of the different clusters in the data set. An example of this type of algorithm is the binary classification algorithm.

## Soft Clustering

It is a good idea to use a soft clustering algorithm when you are looking to solve a real-time problem. The variables or data points in the data set do not necessarily have to belong to a cluster or class, unlike a hard clustering algorithm. A probability is attached to the likelihood that the input data variable or point will belong to one of the predefined clusters.

Clustering algorithms can also be classified as:

## Flat Clustering

A flat clustering algorithm is where the engineer or data scientist will explicitly define to the machine the many categories or classes it should break the data set into.

## Hierarchical clustering

In hierarchical clustering, the user is not allowed to define the number of clusters that the data set must be broken down into. In this type of algorithm, the machine decides the number of clusters it must break the data into.

Another type of classifying suffering algorithm is based on the model of clustering that the machine learning model uses. This is because a task of clustering is subjective. The following classification will shed some light on the different approaches to clustering that engineers or experts like to use.

**Connectivity models**

As the name suggests, these models are based on the assumption that the data points in the data space that are closer to each other will exhibit similar properties when compared to those data points that are farther away. These algorithms will take the following approaches when trying to cluster the input data:

- They will first classify the data points and then proceed to aggregate those points as the distance between the points increases.

- In this step, the partition data are classified as the distance between them will increase.

The distance function is subjective, and it is for this reason that this class of algorithms is not suitable for any scalable function. It cannot handle large data sets. Hierarchical clustering and other variants fall under this category.

**Centroid Models**

Most clustering algorithms are based on identifying the centroid in every cluster. These models will calculate the distance between a data point and the centroid of the cluster. An example of this type of model is the k-means clustering algorithm, and this type of algorithm is heavily dependent on the centroid of the cluster. The user can define the number of clusters that the data can be broken down into, which means that it is important for the user to have some idea of the data set being used in the model. These types of algorithms will run iteratively to identify the centroid of every cluster.

**Distribution Models**

In the distribution model, the classification is based on the probability of the input data. This model is also based on the probability that every data point or variable in the data set will follow the standard normal distribution or the gaussian distribution. These models tend to over fit the data.

**Density Model**

In the density model, the data points or variables in the data set will be plotted on a graph, and the model will decide the cluster that a point should fall into depending on the space in the graph. This variation in density forms the basis of any clustering algorithm. A density algorithm is often used in isolation, and some examples of this model are OPTICS and DBSCAN.

## Implementation of Clustering Algorithms

We will now look at the two types of clustering algorithms – k-means clustering and hierarchical clustering.

### *K-Means Clustering Algorithm*

This type of algorithm is one of the most popular algorithms that engineers use when they want to use a clustering algorithm. The variable 'k' stands for the number of clusters or classes that you want to generate using the given data set. This algorithm is also termed as unsupervised classification.

The user is allowed to define the value of 'k,' and the model will then identify the variables that will fall into a specific class. The model will then calculate the centroid for every cluster of data. This centroid is the center of every cluster, and the number of centroids will be equal to the variable 'k.' You can only use this algorithm if your data set has numerical values.

The advantage of using this algorithm is that it is very easy to understand and simple to build. It is also easy to implement this algorithm on a machine. This is because the model will assign the input data to a cluster automatically, and it is for this reason that this algorithm is used by beginners or amateurs. This is because the user does not have to worry about breaking the data into clusters.

One of the disadvantages of this algorithm is that you will need to define the number of clusters that the algorithm can create. This means that you cannot make any dynamic adjustments if necessary.

The output is also significantly influenced by the data which is fed to the model. The algorithm will tend to convert to local minima, and therefore it is recommended to reset and rerun the algorithm with different seeds to ensure minimal or no error.

It is not a good idea to use this algorithm if you are working with large volumes of data, and it is for this reason that you cannot use this algorithm when it comes to working with real-time applications. It is always a good idea to break down the data into a smaller sample size. This algorithm is very sensitive to outliers, which means that one outlier can affect the accuracy of the model. If the input data has multiple outliers, the response or output variable will be skewed. A solution to this is to use the median value of the clusters instead of the mean.

### *K-means steps of the algorithm*

Randomize and choose the value of 'k,' which is the number of centers of clusters.

Now we should identify a way to assign the data points in the data set into a cluster. This is done using multiple techniques, but the most popular one is to calculate the Euclidean distance. This distance is then used to calculate the centroid of the cluster.

The position of every cluster centroid is updated when every data point or variable has been assigned a cluster. The average of every point in the cluster is the centroid of that cluster.

The second and third steps should constantly be repeated until the model can reach the point of convergence. The point of convergence is the point where every cluster is at the optimal threshold. The remaining iterations will not determine or affect the position of the clusters in the model.

We will now look at how we can build this algorithm in Python (Keen, 2017).

```
#Initialization

import pandas as pd

import numpy as np

import matplotlib.pyplot as plt

%matplotlib inline


df = pd.DataFrame({

    'x': [12, 20, 28, 18, 29, 33, 24, 45, 45, 52, 51, 52, 55, 53, 55, 61, 64, 69, 72],

    'y': [39, 36, 30, 52, 54, 46, 55, 59, 63, 70, 66, 63, 58, 23, 14, 8, 19, 7, 24]

})


np.random.seed(200)

k = 3

#Centroids[i] = [x, y]
```

```
centroids = {
    i+1: [np.random.randint(0, 80), np.random.randint(0, 80)]
    for i in range(k)
}


fig = plt.figure(figsize=(5, 5))
plt.scatter(df['x'], df['y'], color='k')
colmap = {1: 'r', 2: 'g', 3: 'b'}
for i in centroids.keys():
    plt.scatter(*centroids[i], color=colmap[i])
plt.xlim(0, 80)
plt.ylim(0, 80)
plt.show()
```

In [2]:

```
#Assignment Stage
def assignment(df, centroids):
    for i in centroids.keys():
        #sqrt((x1 - x2)^2 - (y1 - y2)^2)
        df['distance_from_{}'.format(i)] = (
            np.sqrt(
            (df['x'] - centroids[i][0]) ** 2
            + (df['y'] - centroids[i][1]) ** 2
            )
        )
    centroid_distance_cols = ['distance_from_{}'.format(i) for i
    in centroids.keys()]
    df['closest']                    =                    df.loc[:,
    centroid_distance_cols].idxmin(axis=1)
    df['closest']       =       df['closest'].map(lambda       x:
    int(x.lstrip('distance_from_')))
    df['color'] = df['closest'].map(lambda x: colmap[x])
    return df
df = assignment(df, centroids)
print(df.head())
fig = plt.figure(figsize=(5, 5))
```

```
plt.scatter(df['x'],    df['y'],    color=df['color'],    alpha=0.5,
    edgecolor='k')
for i in centroids.keys():
    plt.scatter(*centroids[i], color=colmap[i])
plt.xlim(0, 80)
plt.ylim(0, 80)
plt.show()
```

| | x | y | distance_from_1 | distance_from_2 | distance_from_3 | closest | color |
|---|---|---|---|---|---|---|---|
| 0 | 12 | 39 | 26.925824 | 56.080300 | 56.727418 | 1 | r |
| 1 | 20 | 36 | 20.880613 | 48.373546 | 53.150729 | 1 | r |
| 2 | 28 | 30 | 14.142136 | 41.761226 | 53.338541 | 1 | r |
| 3 | 18 | 52 | 36.878178 | 50.990195 | 44.102154 | 1 | r |
| 4 | 29 | 54 | 38.118237 | 40.804412 | 34.058773 | 3 | b |

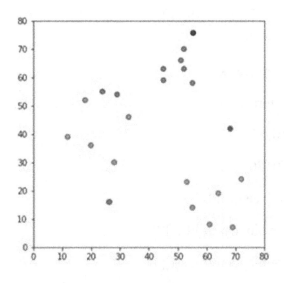

197

In [3]:

```
#Update Stage
import copy
old_centroids = copy.deepcopy(centroids)
def update(k):
  for i in centroids.keys():
    centroids[i][0] = np.mean(df[df['closest'] == i]['x'])
    centroids[i][1] = np.mean(df[df['closest'] == i]['y'])
  return k


centroids = update(centroids)
  fig = plt.figure(figsize=(5, 5))
ax = plt.axes()
plt.scatter(df['x'],    df['y'],    color=df['color'],    alpha=0.5,
edgecolor='k')
for i in centroids.keys():
  plt.scatter(*centroids[i], color=colmap[i])
plt.xlim(0, 80)
plt.ylim(0, 80)
for i in old_centroids.keys():
  old_x = old_centroids[i][0]
  old_y = old_centroids[i][1]
```

dx = (centroids[i][0] - old_centroids[i][0]) * 0.75

dy = (centroids[i][1] - old_centroids[i][1]) * 0.75

ax.arrow(old_x,      old_y,      dx,      dy,      head_width=2, head_length=3, fc=colmap[i], ec=colmap[i])

plt.show()

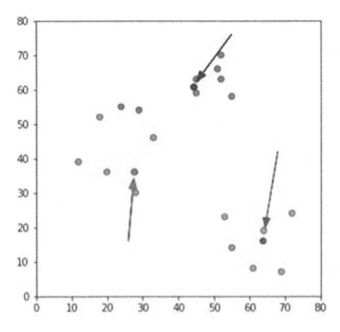

In [4]:

#Repeat Assignment Stage

df = assignment(df, centroids)

#Plot results

fig = plt.figure(figsize=(5, 5))

```
plt.scatter(df['x'],    df['y'],    color=df['color'],    alpha=0.5,
edgecolor='k')

for i in centroids.keys():

    plt.scatter(*centroids[i], color=colmap[i])

plt.xlim(0, 80)

plt.ylim(0, 80)

plt.show()
```

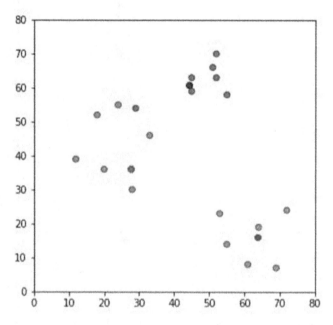

If you look closely at the plot, you will notice that one blue is now red and one red is now green. This means that we are almost at the end of the process. We will repeat this process until there is no change made to the clusters.

In [5]:

```
#Continue until all assigned categories don't change anymore
while True:
    closest_centroids = df['closest'].copy(deep=True)
    centroids = update(centroids)
    df = assignment(df, centroids)
    if closest_centroids.equals(df['closest']):
        break


fig = plt.figure(figsize=(5, 5))
plt.scatter(df['x'], df['y'], color=df['color'], alpha=0.5,
edgecolor='k')
for i in centroids.keys():
    plt.scatter(*centroids[i], color=colmap[i])
plt.xlim(0, 80)
plt.ylim(0, 80)
plt.show()
```

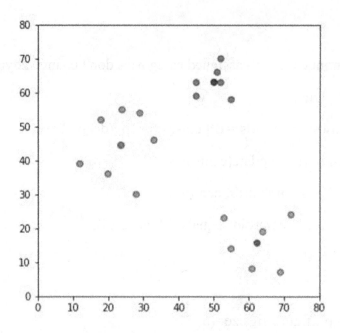

We now have three clusters in the scatter plot and their means are highlighted at the center of the clusters. Let us now look at how we can perform the same action using Scikit-learn.

In [6]:

```
df = pd.DataFrame({

   'x': [12, 20, 28, 18, 29, 33, 24, 45, 45, 52, 51, 52, 55, 53, 55,
61, 64, 69, 72],

   'y': [39, 36, 30, 52, 54, 46, 55, 59, 63, 70, 66, 63, 58, 23, 14,
8, 19, 7, 24]

})


from sklearn.cluster import KMeans
```

```
kmeans = KMeans(n_clusters=3)

kmeans.fit(df)

Out[6]:

KMeans(algorithm='auto',  copy_x=True,  init='k-means++',
max_iter=300,

    n_clusters=3, n_init=10, n_jobs=1,
precompute_distances='auto',

    random_state=None, tol=0.0001, verbose=0)
```

Then we learn the labels

In [7]:

```
labels = kmeans.predict(df)

centroids = kmeans.cluster_centers_
```

In [8]:

```
fig = plt.figure(figsize=(5, 5))

colors = map(lambda x: colmap[x+1], labels)

plt.scatter(df['x'], df['y'], color=colors, alpha=0.5, edgecolor='k')

for idx, centroid in enumerate(centroids):

    plt.scatter(*centroid, color=colmap[idx+1])

plt.xlim(0, 80)

plt.ylim(0, 80)

plt.show()
```

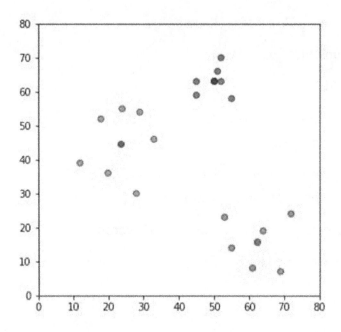

You will obtain a scatter plot based on the code above, and this plot will have four clusters. There will be two clusters at the top of the plot and two at the bottom of the plot. These clusters will overlap each other.

Since you have defined the value of 'k' as 3, there are four clusters that have been created by the model. The model should now calculate the Euclidean distance using the NumPy library that is available in Python.

A new plot is developed after every iteration that helps to provide a visual representation of the data set. Every iteration uses a different centroid for clusters, which means that the centroid will be in a different spot on the graph in every plot. The iterations will continue to run until the model obtains the optimal cluster position.

The Scikit-learn library has a package called sklearn.cluster. This function is used to import the k-means algorithm from the library.

The data points in the k-means algorithm are divided into k-clusters. Each of these cluster cells is called a Voronoi. You must remember the idea of boundaries when it comes to this algorithm since the range of every data set is defined using the boundaries. This helps the machine identify the data points or variables that are outliers.

You can plot the data set on a graph using the following code when you use the Scikit-learn library to build the k-means algorithm.

```
x = [1, 5, 1.5, 8, 1, 9]
y = [2, 8, 1.8, 8, 0.6, 11]
plt.scatter(x,y)
plt.show()
```

You should write the following lines of code if you want to split the data or move it into an array. This should only be done when the graph is plotted. Alternatively, you can convert the data into the required data type.

```
X = np.array([[1, 2],
[5, 8],
[1.5, 1.8],
[8, 8],
[1, 0.6],
```

[9, 11]])

We will initialize the value for k in the code written below. The value of k will determine the number of clusters that you want to split the data into to obtain the results.

```
kmeans = KMeans(n_clusters=2)
kmeans.fit(X)
centroids = kmeans.cluster_centers_
labels = kmeans.labels_
print(centroids)
print(labels)
colors = ["g.","r.","c.","y."]
for i in range(len(X)):
 print("coordinate:",X[i], "label:", labels[i])
 plt.plot(X[i][0], X[i][1], colors[labels[i]], markersize = 10)
plt.scatter(centroids[:, 0],centroids[:, 1], marker = "x", s=150, linewidths = 5, zorder = 10)
plt.show()
```

If you want to obtain accurate results, you should use the k-means ++ algorithm.

## Code for Hierarchical Clustering Algorithm

In a hierarchical clustering algorithm the machine will ensure that the data points or variables in the data set can always be broken down into clusters. The machine will look for those data points that are closest to each other, and develop a dendrogram based on numerous iterations. This dendrogram is a graph where the clusters are plotted on a chart, and the distance between these clusters is calculated. This distance will help the machine calculate the number of clusters within the data set. This algorithm will produce a result that has higher accuracy when compared to the previous algorithm since for the latter the user defines the value of k (Malik, 2018).

```
import NumPy as np


X = np.array([[5,3],
    [10,15],
    [15,12],
    [24,10],
    [30,30],
    [85,70],
    [71,80],
    [60,78],
    [70,55],
    [80,91],])
```

```python
import matplotlib.pyplot as plt

labels = range(1, 11)
plt.figure(figsize=(10, 7))
plt.subplots_adjust(bottom=0.1)
plt.scatter(X[:,0],X[:,1], label='True Position')

for label, x, y in zip(labels, X[:, 0], X[:, 1]):
    plt.annotate(
        label,
        xy=(x, y), xytext=(-3, 3),
        textcoords='offset points', ha='right', va='bottom')
plt.show()
```

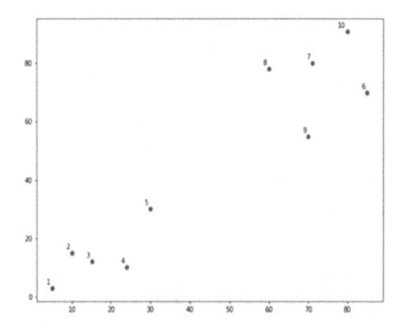

from scipy.cluster.hierarchy import dendrogram, linkage

from matplotlib import pyplot as plt


linked = linkage(X, 'single')


labelList = range(1, 11)


plt.figure(figsize=(10, 7))

dendrogram(linked,

            orientation='top',

            labels=labelList,

```
                    distance_sort='descending',

                    show_leaf_counts=True)

plt.show()


import matplotlib.pyplot as plt

import pandas as pd

%matplotlib inline

import NumPy as np

X = np.array([[5,3],

    [10,15],

    [15,12],

    [24,10],

    [30,30],

    [85,70],

    [71,80],

    [60,78],

    [70,55],

    [80,91],])

from sklearn.cluster import AgglomerativeClustering

cluster = AgglomerativeClustering(n_clusters=2,
    affinity='euclidean', linkage='ward')

cluster.fit_predict(X)
```

```
print(cluster.labels_)
```

Clustering algorithms are a classic example of unsupervised machine learning algorithms. That being said, it can be used with numerous supervised machine learning algorithms to improve the performance and the accuracy of the model.

# Conclusion

Now that we have come to the end of the book, I hope you have gathered a basic understanding of what machine learning is and how you can build a machine learning model in Python. One of the best ways to begin building a machine learning model is to practice the code in the book, and also try to write similar code to solve other problems. It is important to remember that the more you practice, the better you will get. The best way to go about this is to begin working on simple problem statements and solve them using the different algorithms that are mentioned in this book. You can also try to solve these problems by identifying newer ways to solve the problem. Once you get a hang of the basic problems, you can try using some advanced methods to solve those problems.

You should always work towards exploring different functions and features in Python, and also try to learn more about the different libraries like SciPy, NumPy, PyRobotics, and Graphical User Interface packages that you will be using to build different models.

Python is a high-level language which is both interpreter based and object-oriented. This makes it easy for anybody to understand how the language works. You can also extend the programs that you build in Python onto other platforms. Most of the inbuilt libraries in Python offer a variety of functions that make it easier to work with large data sets.

You will now have gathered that machine learning is a complex concept that can easily be understood. It is not a black box that has undecipherable terms, incomprehensible graphs, or difficult concepts. Machine learning is easy to understand, and I hope the book has helped you understand the basics of machine learning. You can now begin working on programming and building models in Python. Ensure that you diligently practice since that is the only way you can improve your skills as a programmer.

Thank you for purchasing the book. I hope it was an enjoyable read for you. You can now spend some time exploring Python and the numerous libraries it has to offer, and see how you can use them to build a variety of machine learning models.

Thank you and all the best!

# References

An introduction to Reinforcement Learning. (2019). Retrieved from
https://medium.freecodecamp.org/an-introduction-to-
reinforcement-learning-4339519de419

Building Machine Learning Models in Python with scikit-learn.
(2019). Retrieved from
https://www.pluralsight.com/courses/python-scikit-learn-
building-machine-learning-models

Code Companion. (2019). Retrieved from
https://codecampanion.blogspot.com/2018/12/learning-
model-building-in-scikit-learn.html

Essential libraries for Machine Learning in Python. (2019).
Retrieved from https://medium.freecodecamp.org/essential-
libraries-for-machine-learning-in-python-82a9ada57aeb

Introduction To Machine Learning. (2019). Retrieved from
https://towardsdatascience.com/introduction-to-machine-
learning-db7c668822c4

Learning Model Building in Scikit-learn : A Python Machine
Learning Library - GeeksforGeeks. (2019). Retrieved from
https://www.geeksforgeeks.org/learning-model-building-
scikit-learn-python-machine-learning-library/

Learning Model Building in Scikit-learn : A Python Machine Learning Library - GeeksforGeeks. (2019). Retrieved from https://www.geeksforgeeks.org/learning-model-building-scikit-learn-python-machine-learning-library/

Practical Tutorial on Data Manipulation with Numpy and Pandas in Python Tutorials & Notes | Machine Learning | HackerEarth. (2019). Retrieved from https://www.hackerearth.com/practice/machine-learning/data-manipulation-visualisation-r-python/tutorial-data-manipulation-numpy-pandas-python/tutorial/

Python Programming Tutorials. (2019). Retrieved from https://pythonprogramming.net/regression-introduction-machine-learning-tutorial/

Python, R. (2019). Pythonic Data Cleaning With NumPy and Pandas – Real Python. Retrieved from https://realpython.com/python-data-cleaning-numpy-pandas/

Pythonic Data Cleaning With NumPy and Pandas – PyBloggers. (2019). Retrieved from http://www.pybloggers.com/2018/03/pythonic-data-cleaning-with-numpy-and-pandas/

Reinforcement learning - GeeksforGeeks. (2019). Retrieved from https://www.geeksforgeeks.org/what-is-reinforcement-learning/

Team, D. (2019). Advantages and Disadvantages of Machine
     Learning Language - DataFlair. Retrieved from https://data-
     flair.training/blogs/advantages-and-disadvantages-of-
     machine-learning/

What Is Unsupervised Machine Learning? | DataRobot. (2019).
     Retrieved from
     https://www.datarobot.com/wiki/unsupervised-machine-
     learning/

www.ingramcontent.com/pod-product-compliance
Lightning Source LLC
Chambersburg PA
CBHW071423050326
40689CB00010B/1959